PENGUIN

THE BARBER OF SEVILLE
THE MARRIAGE OF FIGARO

PIERRE-AUGUSTIN CARON DE BEAUMARCHAIS was born
in Paris in 1732. The son of a clockmaker, he was early appointed
horologist to the French court. A rich marriage established his
fortunes and thereafter he pursued an adventurous career as financial speculator, confidential agent, gun-runner and, ultimately,
man of letters. His literary career began inauspiciously with
Eugénie (1767), an unsuccessful bourgeois drama in the manner of
Diderot, but his numerous lawsuits soon gave him the ammunition for a very successful series of *Mémoires*, in which he attacked his adversaries, establishing his reputation. His most
famous works today, however, are the comedies *The Barber of
Seville* and *The Marriage of Figaro*, which formed the basis of the
operas by Rossini and Mozart. Beaumarchais died in 1799.

JOHN WOOD was born in 1900 and went to Manchester Univer-
sity. After some years in teaching and adult education he spent
his working life in educational administration. Concern with the
relevance of the arts in education, combined with personal predi-
lection, led to involvement with the theatre and with the work of
Molière in particular, as producer and translator. He also translated *The Misanthrope and Other Plays* and *The Miser and Other Plays*
for Penguin Classics.

BEAUMARCHAIS

The Barber of Seville

and

The Marriage of Figaro

Translated with an Introduction by
JOHN WOOD

PENGUIN BOOKS

PENGUIN BOOKS

Published by the Penguin Group
Penguin Books Ltd, 27 Wrights Lane, London W8 5TZ, England
Viking Penguin, a division of Penguin Books USA Inc.
375 Hudson Street, New York, New York 10014, USA
Penguin Books Australia Ltd, Ringwood, Victoria, Australia
Penguin Books Canada Ltd, 2801 John Street, Markham, Ontario, Canada L3R 1B4
Penguin Books (NZ) Ltd, 182–190 Wairau Road, Auckland 10, New Zealand

Penguin Books Ltd, Registered Offices: Harmondsworth, Middlesex, England

This translation first published 1964
15 17 19 20 18 16

Translation copyright © John Wood, 1964
All rights reserved

Printed in England by Clays Ltd, St Ives plc
Set in Monotype Garamond

To Tyrone Guthrie

CONTENTS

๛

'As it is less by my achievement than by my endeavours that I should be judged I still dare to hope for the noble reward I promised myself – the esteem of three great nations, France, America, and even England.'

CARON DE BEAUMARCHAIS

INTRODUCTION

BEAUMARCHAIS is now remembered for his two great comedies and for them, in the English-speaking world at least, because they have won a second and more resounding fame as operas. His other works for the theatre are forgotten, and the vast product of his unflagging energy as a pamphleteer, which gained him an international reputation in his own time, is known only to students. He said himself that he wrote plays *par amusement* – as others found diversion in hunting, intrigue, or love-making. The statement, and any implication that he abstained from the alternative activities mentioned, need not be taken too literally. All the evidence is that he combined, in his work for the theatre, the zest of the amateur with an unremitting and meticulous toil which was wholly professional. Playwriting formed only a part of a life of protean activity, but it was near and dear to his heart, something that he had to do, an essential expression of his personality. He was also, at various times or simultaneously, artisan, courtier, musician, financier, diplomat, merchant and ship-owner, army contractor, secret agent, publisher, litigant, and controversialist on the grand scale: he knew the extremes of success and failure, wealth and poverty, popularity and neglect, the intense life of Paris and the frustrations of exile, the freedom of palaces, and the constraint of jails. At all times he was a man of ideas and one to whom ideas involved action. Glimpses, reflections, echoes of all his activities occur and re-occur in the plays; their enduring interest lies in the degree in which they mirror the age, the society of which and for which they were written, and evoke the love of life, restless energy, unflagging gaiety, audacity, resource, and resilience of their author. It was said of Beaumarchais that he had but one character – himself – and of Figaro that he epitomized all the vices of the man who created him. There is truth in both allegations, but to us who read the plays now it is less a fault than a measure of his achievement.

Beaumarchais was at once a wit and a man of feeling, a lover and a libertine, a paladin and an adventurer: he sounded the clarion of liberty about the walls of the decadent society to which his work lent distinction, and when the time came he defied the powers he had helped to unloose to engulf him. An adventurer, a careerist, a man of no principle – so his enemies described him; brave, warm-hearted, generous to a fault, indefatigable in any cause he undertook to support – so he appeared to his friends; in good fortune and bad he ran true to form.

A man so varied, one so much the epitome of his age, was unlikely to reveal in his work profound truth, the inner realities of human nature. He had not the dimension of his forerunner, Molière, or of his contemporary, Voltaire. The range of his creation was limited and it did not cut deep: indeed, it has been said that his best works, the plays we are concerned with, were no more than pastiche. It is a superficial estimate, but if it were true then what a pastiche! How skilled is the workmanship, how light the touch, how brilliant the finish, how precise the balance of feeling and wit!

That the two plays are now known to the English stage only through Rossini and Mozart is our loss. The repertory of classic comedies does not contain so many works of a like order that we can afford to ignore *The Barber* and *Figaro*. In the European theatre they still hold their place and they have something to say on issues which retain a contemporary interest. Beneath the fun and frivolity there is a quality which is not to be confused with indifference. A man who must laugh at the world lest he should weep is a figure only the happier ages of history can ignore. An ironic awareness of values other than those of conventional society is revealed only in flashes in *The Barber*: in *Figaro* it is implicit, a continuing accompaniment to the comic theme. It is a challenge that the agents of tyranny have rarely failed to detect. Louis XVI, after hearing a reading of *Figaro*, said that such a play could never be allowed to appear on the stage. He did not stand by his estimate, but then he was that type of man. Napoleon's grim comment on Beaumarchais was that in his time such a fellow would have been clapped into jail. And presumably kept there! The restored Bourbons had their censors delete from the plays all reference to censorship. More recent censors have acknowledged in Figaro one who, when speaking of Liberty, does not take that name in vain.

Beaumarchais was born in 1732, the son of a master watchmaker named Caron, himself a most interesting man, a Calvinist turned Catholic, a soldier turned artisan, a provincial settled in Paris, scientifically minded but a lover of music and literature. Pierre Augustin was the seventh of ten children, the only surviving son in a family of six daughters. He had only a limited schooling, but the home life of this talented family was an education in itself, and Beaumarchais, in youth and manhood, read widely in French, English, and Classical literature. At the age of eighteen he ran away from paternal discipline, but returned at his mother's intercession and devoted himself to mastering his craft. Thenceforward his relations with his father were close and affectionate. It was his qualities of intelligence and inventiveness as applied to his craft, of audacity and determination in the face of a threat to his achievement, that first brought the young man to public notice. He had invented a new form of regulator for watches, but his discovery was claimed by one Lepaute, a master watchmaker and *horloger* to the Court. It was the occasion of Beaumarchais's first essay in polemics. Such was the thoroughness with which he documented his protest, the skill and address with which he marshalled his case, that he convinced the Académie des

Sciences of the justice of his claims. At the age of twenty-two he became not only master watchmaker but watchmaker to the King. Thus a career of vaulting ambition was launched. Within a year the young artisan had become a Court functionary, having purchased an office in the Royal Household; within two he had married the widow of his predecessor in his office and gained control of her considerable fortune. It was at this stage that he took the name of Beaumarchais or Caron de Beaumarchais from a small property of his wife. The marriage was unhappily of short duration, and left a legacy of tiresome litigation and the loss of all the fortune that marriage had brought him.

Nothing daunted, apparently, after the briefest of intervals he was exploring another avenue to fortune, exploiting another aspect of his outstanding ability. In 1759 he was teaching the harp to the daughters of Louis XV. He was soon much at home in the inner circles of the Court, an indispensable organizer of gaiety, and turned his contacts to advantage by entering into a close association with Paris Duverney, a financier who had been adviser to Madame de Pompadour and combined banking and farming of royal finance with speculation and promotion of vast projects on his own account. Beaumarchais quickly became rich, and in 1761 purchased one of the secretaryships in the Royal Household, a sinecure which carried formal admission to the nobility. He next attempted to crown this career by obtaining the post of Grand Maître des Eaux et Forêts, but he had to content himself with the deputy Capitainerie de la Varenne du Louvre – the keepership of the Royal Warren. This feudal survival carried certain judicial functions which he continued to exercise, except for intervals when he was abroad, for the next twenty years, even when he was himself at odds with the royal judiciary.

Beaumarchais was now thirty years of age and could well consider that he had done pretty well for himself. At the same

time success had made him numerous enemies, as he was to
find as soon as there was a check to his fortunes. Such upstarts
drew the fire of the less fortunate without securing recognition on equal terms from the old nobility among whom they
mixed in Court circles.

In May 1764 Beaumarchais left his lieutenancy to be exer-
cised by his principal and departed for Spain. His declared
purpose was to vindicate the honour of his sister, Marie
Louise, who had been jilted in Madrid by a writer named
Clavijo. Beaumarchais was later to blow up this domestic
quarrel into a European sensation and make the name of the
unfortunate Clavijo a byword. Goethe in Weimar, Marsollier
in Paris, were to put versions of the story on the stage, and
Beaumarchais himself used parts of it in his own play,
Eugénie. But this was in the future and, immediately, Beaumarchais had other business in Spain. He was engineering,
probably in partnership with Duverney, a vast project for the
exploitation of the Spanish colony of Louisiana by importing
slaves and trading in tobacco. At the same time he was involved in schemes to supply the Spanish armies with munitions and the heir to the Spanish throne with a French mistress,
who was to be an instrument of French policy. Subsidiary
activities included establishing his brother-in-law in business
in Spain, collecting his father's debts, and beginning his cor-
respondence with Voltaire. The major enterprises came to
nothing, but the experience in Spain was to furnish the
Spanish local colour of his plays.

It was to the theatre that Beaumarchais turned on his return
to France. *Eugénie*, his first play, was produced by the Comédie
Française in 1767. It was published in the same year with a
prefatory essay on the *Genre dramatique sérieux*. A sentimental
drama – something, as Beaumarchais said, between heroic
tragedy and true comedy – it was influenced by Diderot,
whose *Père de famille* Beaumarchais had greatly admired. It

was coldly received, hurriedly refurbished, and, in spite of hostile criticism, enjoyed a considerable success. An English version was put on by Garrick in 1769 as *The School for Rakes*. It was followed five years later by *Les Deux Amis ou le négociant de Lyon*, another essay in the sentimental manner which was a failure.

Meanwhile Beaumarchais had married again. The lady was a widow and rich, but this marriage, like the first one, was tragically short-lived, and the son by the marriage did not long survive his mother. In the same year, 1770, Beaumarchais sustained a further blow in the death of his partner, Paris Duverney. This led to disasters which threatened to end his career and did permanently impair his reputation. Duverney's executor, Count de la Blache, denied Beaumarchais monies due from the estate and sued him for debts, which, he alleged, were owed to it. La Blache lost the first round, but the verdict was reversed on appeal. So began a legal process which was to drag on for ten years. In a series of *Mémoires* against Goëzman, who had decided against him, Beaumarchais began by challenging an unjust and corrupt decision. He ended by arraigning at the bar of public opinion the whole judicial system and the ministers who maintained it. The *Mémoires* employ every resource of reasoned argument and rhetoric, of narration, innuendo, wit, and appeal to sentiment. They were eagerly read wherever a literate public existed. The case was the news of the day in London and in Berlin, at the courts of St Petersburg and Schönbrunn. 'What a man,' said Voltaire. 'He has everything – pleasantry, seriousness, reason, vigour, pathos, eloquence of every kind, and yet he strives after none of them. . . .' Horace Walpole, more restrained, as became a good Englishman, was also more perspicacious – 'The man is exceedingly adroit, reasons well and his jests are often amusing – but he is too pleased with himself.'

Though the Goëzman affair added to the gaiety of nations,

it was a deadly ordeal for Beaumarchais, the long-awaited opportunity for his enemies, the testing-time for his courage. The result of La Blache's success on appeal was that Beaumarchais was condemned to pay up; his house and goods were impounded; his late wife's relatives, even his first wife's, disinterred old claims upon him and vilified him without mercy. Moreover, he was not only the victim of civil process but branded as a criminal and sentenced to deprivation of civil rights by the Parlement. When he came into collision on a personal matter with a highly placed but erratic member of the nobility, the Duc de Chaulnes, he was summarily thrown into jail at a time when the case against Goëzman was at its most critical stage. Production of his play *The Barber of Seville*, which was to have taken place in 1773, had to be postponed because no one in the theatre could afford to give a man in his position open support. But Beaumarchais was never so dangerous as when his back was to the wall. Undismayed by the threat of disaster, he carried the fight to the enemy – accused Goëzman and his wife of corruption and continued to put his case to the public with unflagging wit, clarity, and good humour. In court he showed the same qualities combined with remarkable self-control and adroitness. When his enemies resorted to mud-slinging they found their methods recoiled upon them: allegations were made about the famous journey to Spain; Beaumarchais told the whole truth as he saw it, used the hapless Clavijo as the archetype of his enemies, and presented his own loyalty to his sister as evidence of what manner of man he was. As for Goëzman, whose method had been from the first to brand Beaumarchais as a liar and forger, Beaumarchais attacked him first through his wife – the facts of the case gave him no option – and then by disinterring his own personal record with deadly effect. Justice was shown as corrupt and the judge as immoral and devoid of all scruple. When a reluctant judiciary in effect admitted the justice of the case as pleaded by Beaumarchais by finding Goëzman and his wife guilty, Beaumarchais became a popular hero. It was regarded as only a minor flaw in his triumph that he himself was declared at fault too – presumably because he had the audacity to challenge justice at all! He continued to be deprived of civil rights and, much as he enjoyed being lionized, he felt the continuing slur keenly and the road to rehabilitation remained long and hard. It finally came in 1778.

For most men such a case would have been sufficient preoccupation, and there were indeed times when Beaumarchais was too desperate to think of anything else, but, except in mid-crisis, he continued to conduct his multifarious activities. In 1774 he was in London, his plans to produce *The Barber* temporarily put aside. His business was to suppress or destroy certain scandalous chronicles of the youth of Madame Dubarry which an *émigré* Frenchman was threatening to publish. Success in this venture he hoped would secure the favourable intervention of Louis XV and restoration of his civil rights. He was to be disappointed. He returned to France to find the King dying and a successor to whom services in the cause of the Dubarry were the reverse of recommendation. Louis XVI began with a prejudice against the Beaumarchais of the *Mémoires* which he never entirely lost, notwithstanding assiduous service rendered to the Crown. He, Beaumarchais, was in London again in 1775 on a secret mission – and in Germany and Vienna on what appears to have been a wild-goose chase; he returned to London in 1775 and 1776 on the strange business of the Chevalier d'Éon, a celebrity of uncertain sex, formerly a French agent, who possessed documents which it was necessary in the national interest to recover. From these comings and goings Beaumarchais gained little reward and uncertain credit – but an understanding of English politics which he was to turn to account in the cause of the Americans.

He had returned to the theatre in 1775 and triumphantly

after many false starts. *The Barber of Seville* was originally completed as a comic opera in 1772. It was offered to the Opéra Comique and refused. Rewritten as a play in five acts, it was submitted to the censor in 1773 and approved, but Beaumarchais was then in For L'Évêque as a result of the affair of the Duc de Chaulnes. On his release he returned to his plans, but his clashes with the judiciary had strengthened his enemies, and it was known or suspected that the play was to make reference to his experiences as a litigant. Performance was forbidden. On his return from London in 1775 he revised and extended the play. It finally appeared on 23 February 1775 and was received with a chorus of derision – to reappear two days later, remodelled in four acts, and a triumphant success. It has remained in the repertory of the Comédie Française ever since. In England it appeared within less than a year in a translation by Elizabeth Griffith, and performances quickly followed in most European languages. In 1785 it was played at Versailles with the Queen as Rosine and the King's brother, the Count of Artois, as Figaro. It was produced as an opera – the earlier version by Paisello in St Petersburg in 1780 and in the adaptation by Sterbini with music by Rossini in 1816.

In the year of *The Barber*, 1775, Beaumarchais had found a new outlet for his energies and revealed new abilities, new reserves of insight, persistence, and courage in a cause which, in the end, he persuaded his king and his country to make their own. It was from London in this year, while he was engaged in the affair of the Chevalier d'Éon, that he addressed the first of his remarkable letters to Louis XVI on the revolt of the American Colonies and the possibilities offered to France by England's difficulties.

Sire [he wrote in September 1775], the Americans, resolved to go to any lengths rather than yield, and filled with the same enthusiasm for liberty which has so often made the little Corsican nation formidable to Genoa, have 38,000 men under the walls of Boston

... all who were engaged in the fisheries which the English have destroyed have become soldiers ... all who were concerned with maritime trade which the English have forbidden have joined forces with them ... the workers in the ports and harbours have swelled this angry array ... and I say, Sire, that such a nation must be invincible.

It was a bold prophecy, and the King and the French Government were less perspicacious or more cautious than Beaumarchais, but he was not the man to wait upon others for action. In 1776 he raised a loan of a million *livres* and formed a company, Rodrigue Hortalez et Cie, to give succour in the form of arms and munitions to the insurgent colonials. The French and Spanish Governments secretly contributed similar sums. In that year the Americans sent an envoy, Silas Deane, to France to obtain military supplies. He was received at Versailles in a friendly manner, and though no open support was given him, he was put in touch with a secret agent of the Government. The direct result of their negotiations was that during the spring of 1777 ammunition, guns, and complete military equipment for 25,000 men, amounting in value to not less than five million French *livres*, were landed on the American coast. The timely arrival of these supplies permitted the vigorous carrying out of the campaign of 1777, which ended in the decisive victory of Saratoga.* The agent, the organizer, the shipper, was Beaumarchais, and a great deal of the money involved was his own. The credit for having persuaded the French Government to go as far as it did was primarily his. Thus, before the tide of battle had turned, before Franklin had landed in France, before Lafayette raised his volunteers, before Louis and his minister Vergennes had brought their courage to the sticking-point, Beaumarchais had come to grips with the problem, made his dispositions, organized the

* Elizabeth Kite, *Beaumarchais and the War of American Independence*, Boston, 1918.

financial backing – and dispatched his privately chartered fleets through the screen of English cruisers as successfully as he had side-tracked the inquiries of the English Ambassador at Versailles. The full extent of the part played by Beaumarchais in enlisting sympathy, in mobilizing support and influencing the negotiations which finally led to French recognition of the colonies, was not known until long after his death – not until after the French archives of this period were made available in 1886. It is now beyond question and acknowledged on both sides of the Atlantic that the services he rendered to the American cause were not exceeded by any of his countrymen. The passion for liberty and the success of the cause of those whom, to the end of his life, he called 'My friends, the free men of America' had to be their own reward. He recovered from the Americans in his lifetime not one penny of the sums he had expended in their cause. The loan amounting to a million *livres* he had raised on his own security at the instance of the Crown was repaid to him in 1778 to save him from bankruptcy, but Congress showed a lack of scruple, or unawareness of obligations, in dealing with creditors that accorded ill with the nobility of the sentiments it professed in other connexions. Beaumarchais, in poverty during the years of the Revolution, made great efforts to obtain material recognition of the debt owing to him, but in vain. It was not until 1865 that tardy and partial restitution was made to his heirs.

While conducting his war on behalf of the Americans, Beaumarchais was involved in campaigns nearer home. The success of *The Barber* led to a collision with the actors of the Théâtre Français, whose interest in the plays they performed had by custom become most unjustifiably extended. They claimed that after the takings on any night fell below a certain figure the rights in all subsequent performances reverted to them. Exhaustion of the author's interest in his own work they were in the habit of arranging – by giving a performance on an unsuitable occasion or by contriving a clash with some other compelling attraction. This trick they endeavoured to play upon Beaumarchais, but they misjudged their man. He challenged their claims, demanded accounts they were unable or unwilling to produce, appealed to the King's administrator of the theatre, organized his fellow dramatists, and made the facts public with his usual energy. In the end, though the final result was long delayed, the actors were confounded and the rights of authors placed on an equitable and enduring foundation.

Voltaire died in 1778, and in the following year Beaumarchais purchased all his manuscripts, thus forestalling the agents of Catherine the Great. At Kehl, across the Rhine from Strasbourg and so beyond the reach of the censors of the monarchy he was serving in other capacities, he established a publishing house. Type was purchased in England, paper mills set up in Alsace, and the Société Littéraire Typographique established to bring out a full, definitive, and uncensored edition of the works of the master. During the next years the work was pushed ahead with characteristic energy and indifference to expense.

In 1784, on 27 April, when France was once more at peace but the shadows of civil disaster were lengthening, the climax of Beaumarchais's career as a dramatist was reached with the first performance of *La Folle Journée ou le mariage de Figaro*. The idea of the play went back at least as early as *The Barber*. There were references to the family affairs of Figaro in the preface to that play, and it seems probable that Beaumarchais had completed it more or less as we know it as early as 1778; it was accepted by the Comédie Française in 1781. Nevertheless, it was three years before it was publicly performed. It was first approved by the censor with minor modifications, but, rumours of its satirical content having got around, a reading was arranged at Court with the connivance of friends of the

Queen. The scheme went astray. Louis XVI, appalled by the play's impertinences, declared that it could never be performed. This was sufficient advertisement in certain quarters, and Beaumarchais received innumerable requests for private readings. He was not loath to comply, but at the same time he was prudent enough to edit the text, transfer the setting to Spain, and submit it again to the censor. Approval was refused. Arrangements were made for members of the Comédie Française to give the play in the hall of the Menus Plaisirs in honour of the King's brother, the Count of Artois, but at the last moment it was forbidden. A semi-private performance was successfully carried through in the presence of members of the royal family in September 1783, but what Beaumarchais wanted was the approbation of the theatre-going public of Paris, and nothing less would content him. A fourth censor condemned the play, a fifth approved with reservations, a sixth approved unconditionally, and in 1784 permission was obtained from the King himself.

The opening night of the play, long awaited and publicized, was one of the great social occasions of the reign.

All Paris [says Loménie] from the earliest morning thronged the doorways of the Théâtre Français, ladies of the highest rank dining in the dressing-rooms of the actresses in order to be sure of their places. The guards were overwhelmed, the doors broken in, the railings gave way before the pressure of the crowds, and when the curtain rose upon the scene, the finest collection of talent the Théâtre Français ever possessed was there with but one thought to bring out the best of a comedy, flashing with wit, carrying one away in its movement and audacity which, if it shocked some of the boxes, enflamed and electrified the pit.

It began at five-thirty and ended at ten.

The play ran for sixty-eight successive performances, the gross receipts amounting to 347,000 *livres*, the greatest success of the century. Beaumarchais gave his share, some 41,000 *livres*, to charity – a gesture by no means universally appreciated. At this high-water mark of success he had a sharp reminder of the arbitrary nature of royal power. Something he had said about the difficulties of getting it upon the stage – 'that he had had to dare lions and tigers' – was carried to the King and represented as criticism of himself and the Queen. The hero of the day was summarily consigned to St Lazare, a house of correction for delinquent youth. Within five days he was free again, and the first performance after his release was the occasion of a great demonstration of sympathy by an audience which included most of the King's ministers.

In 1786 Mozart's opera was first heard in Vienna. London had not been behindhand.

Finding it impossible to obtain a copy in the original French, though a journey was made to Paris for that purpose, a copy was taken from memory only in the course of eight or nine performances ... furnished with plot, incidents, entrances, exits and some occasional hints ... the remainder was the work of a young Frenchman whose talents and heart are an ornament and an honour to his country.

It was played at the Theatre Royal, Covent Garden, on 21 February 1785 and published in Holcroft's 'translation' in the same year.

In 1786 Beaumarchais made his third marriage. The bride was Mlle Willermawlas, by whom he had had a daughter, Eugénie, in 1777. Whatever may have been the motive on previous occasions, this was at least 'a kind of loving'. His wife stood by him staunchly in the years of affliction which were to come, and survived him.

The triumph of *Figaro* was followed three years later by a production no less dear to Beaumarchais's heart, the long-meditated opera or *drame chanté*, *Tarare*, with music by Salieri, a pupil of Gluck. It had a considerable success and continued to be performed occasionally until the middle of the next cen-

tury. It was not his last work for the theatre, but it marks the
end of his material success. The world Beaumarchais had
known was dissolving. The citadels of power and privilege
were under attack from new men and by methods that were
not his. When he became involved in new litigation and
polemical exchanges he found that there was no lack of new
enemies eager to use his own weapons against him, to revive
old scandals and defame his past, and that he was now the
more vulnerable in that he was successful, in good standing
with authority, and, what is more, rich. Had he not, therefore,
exploited the people? The great house which he was building
for himself near the Bastille was to do him no good. He who
was still mistrusted in Court circles as a *parvenu*, an adventurer, a man of dangerous ideas, was to the new men a creature
of the régime they were determined to destroy. In vain he pro-
tested his services to his country, demonstrated his generosity
to the people. His motives were suspect. He saw old friends
and old enemies alike fleeing into exile or taking the road to
the scaffold. He became involved in a scheme for securing for
French use a store of muskets which were beyond the frontier
in the Low Countries. His frustrations in the effort to recover
them had a nightmare quality: while minister succeeded minister at home and allegiances changed bewilderingly abroad he
was alternately encouraged and thwarted, trusted and suspected, finally sent abroad and denounced as an *émigré* for
having gone. His wife, sister, and daughter were thrown into
jail and his possessions confiscated in his absence. He moved
from the Low Countries to England, from England to Ham-
burg, where he lived for some months in poverty, increasingly
deaf, among people whose language he did not speak. Yet
though régimes changed and fortune proved fickle, he remained the same Beaumarchais. When, in 1792, he was ad-
vised to show discretion, he replied publicly with characteristic indifference to consequences, 'Into what dreadful sort of

liberty are we fallen, worse than real slavery if a man who is guiltless of any offence must defer to the power of those who have really offended because they have it in their power to destroy him.' In the end they did not destroy him. He survived prison, proscription, and exile and returned in 1796 to build his fortunes again. The following year he saw his last play, *La Mère coupable*, performed by the former actors of the Théâtre Français. He heard once more the applause of audiences and enjoyed reunion with his family and intimate friends. He was still planning new activities when he died suddenly of apoplexy in 1799, the year of the establishment of the Consulate. He was sixty-seven.

The Barber of Seville

The origins of *The Barber of Seville* have been traced to one of the *Parades* which Beaumarchais wrote for the house theatricals at Étiolles about 1761. Parts of the play as we know it still bear the stamp of farcical improvisation; for example, the scene of La Jeunesse and L'Éveillé. The interpolation of the songs which gave offence to the purists of the Théâtre Français probably had a like origin. It is not surprising that Beaumarchais first thought of this work in operatic terms: he was a lover of music, and particularly of popular music, and had taken great pleasure in collecting the songs and dances of Spain. Some of the songs in *The Barber* were set to popular tunes; for others he composed the music himself. When the Opéra Comique refused it he rewrote it as a play.

Almost nothing in the plot or the range of characters is original. The sub-title goes back to Scarron (1610–60), the main idea of the plot – the old man foiled by young love – to Molière and the *École des femmes* if no earlier. What is new is the dimension of the characterization, above all of that of Figaro. Beaumarchais himself says that it is Figaro who determines the character of the play. Its liveliness, its variety of action, do not depend on the plot, which is basically simple, but on the opposition of characters a stage nearer to life than those of traditional comedy. Figaro is clearly the lineal descendant of Scapin, and the unnumbered scoundrelly valets back to Plautus and the New Comedy. He is new in that he transcends the type. He has a past and a future, an incalculable quality, resources not strictly necessary to the action, contradictory elements in his character, and, in this play and its successors, he changes and develops. Beaumarchais suggests that because Bartholo is less of a fool than dupes in comedy usually are he requires more resource to outwit him, and so provokes movement within the plot. This may be so, but the reverse is certainly true. Figaro provokes a dislike in Bartholo which goes beyond what is necessary to the plot. It has a distinct and personal flavour. Similarly, Figaro sharpens our impressions of Almaviva and of Rosine. Almaviva would be no more than the conventional young lover did we not see him in relation to Figaro in the master-and-man exchanges which are new not in basic conception but in treatment. It is in her relations with Figaro that Rosine's ingenuous charm is most truly revealed.

Characteristic of Beaumarchais here and in *The Marriage of Figaro* is the lightness of touch. Almaviva may be old in the ways of gallantry, but we are persuaded that what he runs after may be true happiness after all. There are equivocal elements in Rosine, and some contemporary critics did not hesitate to stigmatize her morals as lax, but to those who will give themselves to the mood of the play her faults become peccadilloes and the end justifies all Figaro's means.

The element of social comment has always been emphasized, but it is doubtful whether anyone who knew nothing of Beaumarchais or his times would detect it today. To the contemporary audience it abounded in innuendo, references to contemporary people, and the version which appeared on the first night was evidently even more topical. Figaro, to the Parisian audience of the day, was Beaumarchais in person, the impudent adventurer, cocking a snook at authority, puffing his wares, flaunting his opinions, and using the theatre to redress the balance of his fortunes in real life. Molière always denied that his characters represented real people. Beaumarchais made no secret of the fact that he put references to real people and real life into the mouths of his characters; no contemporary had any doubt, for example, that Brid'oison in *The Marriage of Figaro* was not merely the personification of the fatuity of judicial procedure but the arch-enemy, Goëzman himself. Bazile's evocation of calumny was calumny as Beaumarchais had suffered from it when the storm broke upon him after the decision of the Parlement de Maupeou. Even the reference – among Bartholo's prejudices – to *drames* was not to *drames* in general but to Beaumarchais's own unsuccessful *drames* in particular.

Technically the play is tighter and more consistent in construction than *The Marriage of Figaro*, more manageable for the theatre, shorter in cast and playing time. There are few comedies so engaging, with such abundance of wit and careless inconsequence. It speaks for the young Beaumarchais, still carefree and fun-loving, for whom precaution was futile in spite of fortune's vicissitudes.

The Marriage of Figaro

The Marriage of Figaro is that rare occurrence in literature, a true sequel. The freshness and vigour of the earlier work are carried over into the new, the characters are recognizably the same, but time has not stood still in Andalusia – or in France. There is still laughter and gaiety and wit in the world of Aguas Frescas – as at the Court of Versailles – but there are disillusion and weariness and awareness that happiness cannot necessarily be won by pursuing it. The mood is still one of irresponsibility – life for the day and its follies – but there are undertones of discontent, a murmur from the world outside the theatre. Figaro is not the only one to answer back now. There is Antonio, even if he is tipsy, and there are the speeches of Marceline, even though the actors suppressed them.

Figaro is still young – young enough to be in love but old enough to know and have doubts of his luck. His wit is still undulled, but it is now more often ironic. His cynicism is becoming misanthropy, his social impertinence social criticism. The flippant responses of *The Barber* – 'How many masters would pass muster as valets?', 'Aren't the poor to be allowed any faults?' – did no more than give new piquancy to the old master-and-servant relationship: they were little more significant in their context than the usual lover-and-confidant exchanges. Now things are different. Master and man were in the earlier play working in concert: now they are in opposition, and behind the conventions of privilege we see that this is a game where the better man will win. The better man isn't the master, and the better man knows it. Figaro is not what he was: nor is the count. He is bored as the great men of Versailles were bored. Vanity and self-indulgence are his sole motives and the end is no longer one with which the audience sympathizes. Yet Beaumarchais can still endow him with charm. There are occasions when he can take a point laughingly. The old lightness of touch prevents his being detestable as it preserves Rosine from being a mere object of pity. But it is a near thing. The last act is more than a farcical *tour de force*: it tips back the balance to comedy and makes all well that ends well.

In what degree was *The Marriage of Figaro* a daring and political play? Certainly it was so regarded by contemporaries.

The first reactions of Louis XVI have been mentioned. Gudin, the friend and biographer of Beaumarchais, says, 'In this play the *parterre* applauded not only scenes of pure comedy but also the courageous man who dared to comment on and to ridicule the libertinage of great nobles, the ignorance of magistrates, the venality of officials, and the false pleadings of lawyers.' Another contemporary comment was that it was 'the end of the old order'. Napoleon said that it was 'the revolution in action'.

All this does not mean that the play was a revolutionary act, still less that it was so regarded by its author. What Beaumarchais was saying was no more than people in all sections of society were saying and thinking. What he said was effective and exciting in theatrical terms because it was expressed with a pertinence which passed as impertinence. This is not to say that Beaumarchais was not sincere. That the feelings expressed by Figaro, the criticisms of privilege which are inherent in the play, were wholly those of its author, no one familiar with his work as a whole can doubt. There is no social criticism in the plays which is not implied also in the *Mémoires* and often put more specifically. The whole life of Beaumarchais was an assertion of individuality against the constraints of social privilege, an anticipation of the demand for the opening of careers to ability: his conduct on innumerable public and private occasions was evidence of a humanity which reacted on impulse to cruelty or oppression. Being what he was, he wrote that kind of play, but there is no evidence that he considered himself as a destroyer of the social order or political institutions. He was personally loyal, indeed obsequious, in his relations with the Crown: what he felt about his dealings with great men and ministers comes out in the speeches of Figaro, but this is all very far from being political. Of the dangers of political licence he was, in fact, well aware. He wrote of England in 1775:

The unhappy English people with its restless craving for liberty would inspire something like compassion in anyone who considered their condition. They despise us as slaves because we obey voluntarily ... but the licentious passion which the English call liberty never gives this untameable people a moment of happiness or true repose.

He did not foresee that a licentious passion for liberty was a danger to his own country and that the danger was inherent in the denial of ordered expression of that passion, but he was not alone in this. Nor was he alone in being able to feel the true pulse of liberty in America without recognizing its implications for France. At all times he was inclined to overvalue the effectiveness of argument and the power of reason, and to idealize the 'natural' emotions of ordinary men and women as opposed to the selfish passions of the great. But in this he was of his age and the illusion was not an ignoble one.

Marceline's speeches in Act Three which the actors wished to have omitted and Beaumarchais restored in the published version involve an ambivalence of another kind. They are of great interest as expressions of a new attitude to women, but they are dramatically out of place, intrusions from another convention. They threaten to overbalance the play into sentiment and sentimentality. Marceline is indeed a curiously inconsistent piece of characterization. In *The Barber* she is a person known to us only by report. In the early part of *The Marriage of Figaro* she is the comic rival to Suzanne, a farcical duenna. She assumes a new dimension and a quite different personality when she is revealed as the long-lost mother, the victim of Bartholo, and the personification of virtue betrayed. Beaumarchais seems to have known a great deal more about his characters than he revealed in the plays – there are new revelations to come in *La Mère coupable* – but what he tells of Marceline is inadequate. The actors were right; the part is unplayable without cutting and the note given by

Beaumarchais in the preface to the published edition, that the actress playing the part should rise to the height of the noble opportunities of the revelation scene, is nonsense. It is, however, a sort of nonsense which was very much of the period and to which Beaumarchais had very strong loyalties. He was the contemporary of Rousseau as well as of Voltaire and the lifelong admirer of Richardson. *Pamela* set his standards of womanly virtue, or one set of standards – those which he expected to apply in novels and plays. Fortunately he was also able to create and appreciate Suzanne, a character completely outside the range of the *drame sentimental* – though in the last of his plays we find her with Figaro in just such a setting.

A practical difficulty of the play on the stage is its length. Four and a half hours must have been long even for an audience which looked for more from the theatre than passive entertainment. For a modern performance some cutting is inevitable, but any attempt at cutting reveals how much more closely knit the play is than appears at first sight. There is a constant variation in the focus of interest, but the thread of the story is unbroken from first to last. The play may be compared to a firework display in the grand manner, where one set-piece after another bursts into activity, but before we are aware that any one has died down another is in eruption, and while our interest is diverted the cunning artificer has refitted the first so that it can spark off again into a new shower of activity. While the rivalry of Figaro and his master is never quiescent, our attention is temporarily diverted by the passages between the Countess and Chérubin, the Countess and the Count, Figaro and Marceline, and finally Figaro and Suzanne, and all come into simultaneous activity at the one central point in the end.

It is, with the exception which has been referred to, a masterpiece of unity in intricacy, a display of virtuosity in which the essentials are never obscured, plot, personal comment and basic characterization all maintained in balance and in accord.

The Dramas

Eugénie, *The Two Friends*, and *The Guilty Mother* span a period of thirty years, with the two comedies and *Tarare* separating the second from the third. It is clear that although Beaumarchais abandoned the *drame sérieux* after the failure of *The Two Friends*, this kind of play answered to some deep feeling in him. It is not just a question of moral seriousness which, as has been mentioned, crops up incongruously in *Figaro*, but of the bourgeois element which was a part of Beaumarchais and his age. He aspired to success, and success in his day was measured in aristocratic terms, but he was very conscious of his bourgeois virtues, love of his father, of his home, devotion to his sisters, his daughter, his humbler friends. This was part of the man, and in this respect no one was ever less spoiled by success. But in his work the cult of feeling had less fortunate results. *Eugénie* is not the worst play of its kind, but it is wholly contrived, an exercise to produce a given result – virtue coming to terms with vice – on a known model, and psychologically unconvincing. In *The Two Friends* the characters are even more stilted, the motivation is even less probable, and the idea behind the choice of plot, though an interesting anticipation of much of nineteenth-century drama, is realized in terms so arbitrary – honesty being made to pay dividends, moral and material – as to deny the play even such theatrical qualities as *Eugénie* had.

In *The Guilty Mother* Beaumarchais returns to his earlier manner, redeems a promise to continue the fortunes of the Almaviva household, and, by implication, challenges comparison with Molière, since the alternative title is *The Other Tartuffe*. At this distance it is difficult to understand how the

Beaumarchais who defended the Countess from the prurient
critics who took a narrow view of her relations with Chérubin
can present her twenty years later as guilty, though repentant –
but that is what happens. Léon and Florestine, the star-
crossed lovers of the play, are the illegitimate children of
Rosine and the Count respectively, and it is their illegitimacy
which provides the fortunate denouement and saves us and
them from the alternative of incest. We see Suzanne and
Figaro supplanted as motivators of the plot by the new Tartuffe, a double-dyed villain of melodrama. There are scenes of
considerable dramatic force, but wit gives place now to sentiment and invention to contrivance. Contrivance may be toler-
able where the purpose is to provoke the audience to laughter,
but it is less so when the object is to move it to tears. Moreover, the tears are not those provoked by the inhumanity of
the real world but by the false dilemmas of theatrical villainy.
Nevertheless, the play had considerable success. Beaumarchais himself took great pleasure in it and it was the forerunner of many guilty mothers, repentant husbands, and
happy issues from contrived afflictions.

Beaumarchais as Innovator

Considering that Beaumarchais was not primarily or solely a
man of the theatre, it is remarkable that he was able to give
such effective attention as he did to practical details and to
make contributions which were new. Comedy in his time was
not the most highly regarded theatrical form. The preference
was for tragedy, though little of lasting value was produced in
response to the preference. The attempts Beaumarchais made
to further the intermediate form – the drama of sentiment –
and to draw upon bourgeois life for material were not a success, but they set precedents which were important for the
future. Not only the melodrama but the social comedy of the

nineteenth century and the twentieth go back to his *drame sérieux*. His innovations in comedy were considerable. He broke the pattern which since the days of Molière had become increasingly formal. He restored farce and fun to the theatre and to the Théâtre Français. He returned to the precedent set by Molière of using prose, and his prose was a spoken version of the language. The critics deplored his indifference to style, but to achieve a colloquial effect was what he intended. His characters speak as in life to themselves and to others with as little resort to convention as any speech heard in the theatre until modern times. The dialogue is theatrical only in that the characters speak for effect and with point. There is no rhetoric and little artificiality. Even the songs are introduced naturally, and they are, in general, popular.

Beaumarchais was particularly alive to visual effects. He gives directions as to costume and to positioning at critical moments. He was very much aware of the importance of casting to character rather than to convention. For example, for the Countess in *Figaro* he chose Mlle Saint Val, who had made her reputation as a tragic actress. For Suzanne he chose Mlle Contat, who was not previously regarded as a *soubrette* but thoroughly justified the decision. In the part of Chérubin, written for a boy, he himself explains that he had to take a girl. His choice fell upon Mlle Olivier, an English girl, in place of the more celebrated Mlle Rémont, who had played it in the earlier semi-private performances.

His comments upon the first performances of several of his own plays show evidence of an unusually practical and critical theatrical intelligence, his rapid revisions of his plays on seeing them in performance an acute appreciation of audience reaction.

Beaumarchais in English

As has been mentioned earlier, no time was lost in publishing translations or adaptations of the plays in English. *Eugénie* appeared in English as *The School for Rakes*, translated by Elizabeth Griffith, in 1769. *Les Deux Amis ou le négociant de Lyons*, translated by 'C.H.', was published as *The Liverpool Merchant* in 1800 and was considered sufficiently important to appear in Bell's compendium, *The London Stage*. Elizabeth Griffith's translation of *The Barber* was published in 1776 and there were several reissues before the end of the century, but it was not until 1905 that a second translation was published, that of Myrick (Dent, Temple Dramatists). A new edition appeared in 1949. Samuel French (New York) published a translation by Stewart Robb in 1939. *The Marriage of Figaro* appeared very promptly in Holcroft's adaptation – published in 1785. A second version translated or adapted by Bishop was published in 1809. There appears to have been no other translation published in England.

Biographies of Beaumarchais in English are few, and none does full justice to his character and career. Still less is there any critical appreciation of his plays. The best account of his life is given in Elizabeth Kite's *Beaumarchais and the War of American Independence*. Rivers's *Figaro – the Life of Beaumarchais* (London, 1922) is readable and useful. Another full-length account of Beaumarchais in English, presumably a translation though not so described, is Frischauer's *Beaumarchais – an Adventurer in a Century of Women* (London, 1936). It is very much what its title would suggest. Recently Cynthia Cox's *The Real Figaro* has appeared (Longmans, 1962). It gives a clear and complete account of the main facts of Beaumarchais's life and career, but the thorough critical biography in English remains to be written.

1962   J.W.

The Barber of Seville

The Futile Precaution

CHARACTERS

COUNT ALMAVIVA, a Spanish grandee, in love with
Rosine

FIGARO, barber of Seville

ROSINE, a young lady of noble birth, ward of Bartholo

BARTHOLO, physician and Rosine's guardian

BAZILE, organist and music master to Rosine

WAKEFUL [L'ÉVEILLÉ], servant of Bartholo, a dull
sleepy boy

YOUTHFUL [LA JEUNESSE], an elderly servant of Bartholo

A notary

An alcalde

Alguazils and servants

SCENE: *Seville, first outside Bartholo's house beneath Rosine's
window, and thereafter inside.*

ACT ONE

[COUNT ALMAVIVA *alone, wearing a wide brown cloak, his hat brim turned down. He takes out his watch as he walks up and down.*]

COUNT ALMAVIVA: Not so late as I thought. It's still not quite her usual time for appearing at the lattice. No matter! Better arrive too early than miss the one moment for seeing her. If any of my acquaintance at Court were to spy me now, a hundred leagues from Madrid and hanging about every morning under the windows of a woman I've never even spoken to . . . they'd take me for a Spaniard of Isabella's time. . . . And why not? We all run after happiness, and mine lies in Rosine's affection. But fancy following a woman to Seville when Madrid and the Court offer such a variety of easily won pleasures! That's just what I'm trying to get away from. I'm weary of the conquests that self-interest or habit or vanity present us in unending succession. How delightful it would be to be loved for oneself alone! If only I could feel certain that in this disguise . . . Oh, the Devil take the fellow! What does he want coming just now?

[*The* COUNT *withdraws as* FIGARO *enters, a guitar slung over his shoulder. He is humming cheerfully, pencil and paper in hand.*]

FIGARO [*breaking into song*]:

> Begone dull care
> That ever art
> Man's years and happiness consuming.
> Come wine, good wine,
> That ever doth
> Man's heart illumine.

Not bad so far, eh?

> That ever doth
> Man's heart illumine.
> Let wine and leisure
> Dispute my heart. . . .

No, no, there's no dispute. They are equally at home there.

> Divide my heart and pleasure.

Can one say divide? Oh, Lord, yes! Our good friends who write comic operas don't worry about details like that. Anything that isn't worth saying – they sing nowadays!

> Let wine and leisure
> Divide my heart and pleasure. . . .

I would like to finish up with something witty and sparkling . . . something that sounds really original. [*He goes down on one knee and writes as he sings.*]

> I'll love the one and be happy with the other . . .

Oh dear! That's flat! It isn't . . . I need more contrast – an antithesis!

> The one I'll serve, the other shall serve me
> And so I'll be
> Serving and served in equal measure.

By Jove! That's got it!

> The one I'll serve, the other shall serve me
> And so I'll be
> Serving and served in equal measure.

Well done, Figaro!

[*Singing as he writes:*]

> Let wine and leisure
> Divide my heart and pleasure.
> The one I'll serve – the other shall serve me
> And so I'll be
> Serving and served in equal measure
> Serving and served in equal measure.

Ha, ha! When there's an accompaniment to it we shall see, you gentlemen who decide whether a play succeeds or not, we'll see if I don't know what I'm talking about! [*Noticing the Count*] I've seen that priest before somewhere. [*Rises to his feet.*]

THE COUNT [*aside*]: I seem to know this fellow.

FIGARO [*aside*]: No. He's no priest. That proud and noble bearing . . .

THE COUNT [*aside*]: That grotesque appearance . . .

FIGARO: I'm *not* mistaken. It's Count Almaviva.

THE COUNT: I do believe it's that rascal Figaro.

FIGARO: Himself. My Lord!

THE COUNT: Miserable scoundrel! If you utter a single word . . .

FIGARO: Yes, I recognize you – and the familiar epithets you always condescended to bestow upon me.

THE COUNT: I shouldn't have recognized *you*. You are so fat and sleek. . . .

FIGARO: Well, what do you expect, Sir – it's poverty.

THE COUNT: Poor fellow! But what are you doing in Seville? Didn't I recommend you for a job in a government office?

FIGARO: Yes, and I got it, My Lord, and very grateful I was too.

THE COUNT: Call me Lindor. Don't you see [*indicates his disguise*] that I want to conceal my identity?

FIGARO: I'll be off, then.

THE COUNT: On the contrary. I'm waiting for something here, and two people in conversation are less likely to provoke notice than one walking up and down by himself. Let us appear to be gossiping. Well now, about the job?

FIGARO: On the strength of Your Excellency's recommendation the Minister promptly appointed me to a post as apprentice apothecary.

THE COUNT: What! With an army doctor?

FIGARO: No, with a horse doctor. I was sent to a stud farm in Andalusia.

THE COUNT [*laughing*]: An excellent beginning!

FIGARO: It wasn't a bad job. I was in charge of the drugs and the dressings, so I was able to sell people the medicines intended for the horses.

THE COUNT: And so kill off His Majesty's subjects?

FIGARO: Well now – no remedy is infallible – but they did sometimes cure Galicians, Catalans, and Auvergnats . . .

THE COUNT: Then why did you give it up?

FIGARO: Give it up? It gave me up! Someone reported me to the powers that be. . . .

> 'Pale Envy, she whose clawlike hands . . .'

THE COUNT: Oh, steady on! Do you mean to say you write poetry as well? I noticed you scribbling on your knee as you were singing just now.

FIGARO: That was the very cause of my misfortune, Your Excellency. When it came to the ears of the Minister that I was in the habit of turning out complimentary verses – and very neat they were too, I may say – that I contributed acrostics to the newspapers, and that there were other little trifles of mine going the rounds – in a word, when he learned that I actually appeared in print, he took a very serious view of it and had me sacked out of hand on the pretext that a love of letters was incompatible with ability for business.

THE COUNT: There's something in that. But didn't you make representations to him?

FIGARO: No, I felt I was lucky to hear no more of it – knowing as I did that a great man is doing you pretty well if he's doing you no harm.

THE COUNT: You aren't telling the whole story. I seem to remember that you were a pretty disreputable specimen when you were with me.

FIGARO: Good Heavens, Your Excellency, aren't the poor to be allowed any faults?

THE COUNT: Idle, dissolute . . .

FIGARO: On the basis of the virtues commonly required in a servant does Your Excellency know many masters who would pass muster as valets?

THE COUNT [*laughing*]: Not bad! So you decided to settle down here?

FIGARO: Not immediately . . .

THE COUNT [*interrupting*]: Just a moment . . . I thought there was someone. . . . Go on, tell me the rest.

FIGARO: Back in Madrid I decided to try my literary abilities again. As the theatre seemed to offer a suitable field . . .

THE COUNT: Good Lord!

[*While* FIGARO *goes on talking, the* COUNT *keeps his eyes on the lattice.*]

FIGARO: I really can't understand why I wasn't successful. I filled the pit with a most industrious collection of people. They made good use of their hands and their clappers! I barred canes and gauntlets – anything that didn't provide a loud enough applause! And I'm bound to say that the coffee houses seemed to be well disposed towards me – but it was the *critics* who . . .

THE COUNT: Oh, the critics! Typical disappointed author!

FIGARO: Yes, we are all alike, and why not? They gave me the bird, but if ever I can get them together again I . . .

THE COUNT: You'll bore them to death in revenge, eh?

FIGARO: I have it in for them, by Gad!

THE COUNT: You have, have you? But don't you know that they only allow a condemned man twenty-four hours for cursing his judges?

FIGARO: You get twenty-four years in the theatre – a lifetime's too short to exhaust a resentment like mine.

43

THE COUNT: I like to see you letting yourself go, but you didn't say what made you leave Madrid.

FIGARO: It must have been my good angel, Your Excellency, since I've been so fortunate as to meet my old master again! I realized in Madrid that the so-called Republic of Letters is nothing but a pack of wolves – all constantly at odds with the others. Given over as they are to the mutual hatreds which spring from their ridiculous rivalries, all the various insects, flies, gnats, midges, critics, envious journalists, booksellers, publishers, the whole swarm of parasites attach themselves to the skin of the unfortunate man of letters and succeed in the end in sucking out of him what little bit of life and blood remain to him. So, weary of writing, bored with myself, and disgusted with my fellows, up to the ears in debt and without a penny to my name, convinced at last that the humble rewards of the razor were preferable to the empty honours of the pen, I left Madrid and, with my pack on my back, made my way, philosophically enough, through the two Castiles, La Mancha, Estremadura, Sierra Morena, and Andalusia, welcomed in one place and jailed in the next, but always superior to fortune, praised by some and condemned by others, in fair weather and foul, defying all enemies, laughing at my own misfortunes, and playing the barber to anyone who needed me – here you find me at last established in Seville and at Your Excellency's disposal for any duties for which you care to command me.

THE COUNT: And what taught you such a cheerful philosophy?

FIGARO: Habitual misfortune. I forced myself to laugh at everything for fear of having to weep. What do you keep looking over there for?

THE COUNT: We must hide.

FIGARO: But why?

THE COUNT: Come along, you wretch. You'll ruin everything for me.

[*They hide. The lattice on the first floor opens and* BARTHOLO *and* ROSINE *appear at the window.*]

ROSINE: How pleasant to breathe the fresh air. This lattice is so seldom open. . . .

BARTHOLO: What's the paper you have there?

ROSINE: Some lines from *The Futile Precaution* which my music master gave me yesterday.

BARTHOLO: And what is *The Futile Precaution*?

ROSINE: A new play. .

BARTHOLO: Another drama I suppose! Some new sort of silliness!*

ROSINE: Oh, I know nothing about that.

BARTHOLO: Well, well! The newspapers and the authorities will deal with it for us. What a barbarous age!

ROSINE: You are always blaming the age we live in.

BARTHOLO: Forgive me the liberty! What has it produced that we should praise it? Nonsense of every kind! Liberty of thought, the Force of Gravity, Electricity and Magnetism, universal toleration, inoculation, quinine, the Encyclopedia, and the new-fangled Drama!

[*The paper slips from* ROSINE'S *hand and falls into the road.*]

ROSINE: Oh! My song! My song! It dropped down there while I was listening to you. Run down at once, Sir, or I shall lose my song.

BARTHOLO: Why the deuce can't folks stick to things when they've got 'em. [*Leaves balcony.*]

ROSINE [*looking down and signalling*]: Sst!

[*The* COUNT *appears.*]

Pick it up and get out of sight.

* *Note by Beaumarchais:* Bartholo didn't like dramas. Perhaps he had written a tragedy in his youth.

[*The* COUNT *springs forward, picks up the paper, and returns to his hiding-place.*]

BARTHOLO [*coming out at the street door*]: Where is it? I can't see anything.

ROSINE: Under the balcony. By the wall.

BARTHOLO: A nice sort of job you've given me! Has anyone come past?

ROSINE: I haven't seen anyone.

BARTHOLO [*to himself*]: And I was silly enough to come and look for it! Bartholo, my lad, you are a simpleton. This will teach you never to open a lattice that gives on to the street. [*He goes into the house again.*]

ROSINE [*still on the balcony*]: My unhappiness is my excuse. Alone, confined to the house, subject to the persecution of a man I hate, am I to blame if I endeavour to escape from slavery?

BARTHOLO [*reappearing on the balcony*]: Go inside again, Signora. It's my fault if you've lost your music, but it's a misfortune that shan't occur again. I promise you.

[*He fastens the shutters. The* COUNT *and* FIGARO *re-enter cautiously.*]

THE COUNT: Now that they have gone in we'll have a look at this mysterious song. There's certainly something queer about it. Why! It's a letter!

FIGARO: And he wanted to know what *The Futile Precaution* was!

THE COUNT [*reading excitedly*]: 'Your devotion arouses my interest. As soon as my guardian has left the house sing something or other to this tune – something which will reveal to me the name, estate, and intentions of one who seems to display such constancy in his attachment to the unfortunate Rosine.'

FIGARO [*imitating Rosine*]: My song! My song! It's dropped down there. Oh, run down, Sir, run down. [*He laughs.*] Oh, these women! If you want to see how clever the most artless of women can become – try locking them up!

THE COUNT: My dearest Rosine!

FIGARO: No further need to worry about what you are doing here in disguise. There's love-making in prospect.

THE COUNT: Yes, you know now, but if you gossip . . .

FIGARO: Gossip? Me? I won't waste any of the much-abused and high-sounding phrases about honour and devotion upon you. I can put the position in two words: self-interest. Self-interest will answer for me. Use that as your yardstick and . . .

THE COUNT: Very well. Let me tell you then that six months ago I met by chance on the Prado a young lady . . . as beautiful as . . . but then you've just seen her! I searched the length and breadth of Madrid for her, but in vain. It wasn't until a few days ago that I found that her name is Rosine, that she's of noble birth, an orphan, and married to an elderly doctor called Bartholo, who lives in this very town.

FIGARO: A pretty little bird, I agree. She'll take some flushing! But, who told you she was the doctor's wife?

THE COUNT: Everybody says so.

FIGARO: That's a tale he has made up since he came back from Madrid to put young men off the scent. As yet she's only his ward, but it won't be long before . . .

THE COUNT: Never! But that's good news indeed! I was determined to go to any lengths to condole with her. Now I find that she's free after all! There isn't a moment to lose. I must win her love and frustrate this base alliance that he's planning for her. Do you know him, this guardian of hers?

FIGARO: As well as my own mother.

THE COUNT: What sort of a man is he?

FIGARO [*rattling it off quickly*]: Oh, he's a stoutish, shortish, oldish, greyish, cunning, smarmy, posing, nosing, peeping, prying, creeping, whining, snivelling sort of man.

THE COUNT [*impatiently*]: All right, I've seen him. I mean his character. . . .

FIGARO: Coarse, mean, infatuated with his ward, jealous beyond all measure where she's concerned, and she hates him like poison.

THE COUNT: And his likeable qualities?

FIGARO: He hasn't any!

THE COUNT: So much the better. Is he honest?

FIGARO: Just enough to avoid being hanged.

THE COUNT: Better still. To punish a rogue and at the same time achieve one's own happiness . . .

FIGARO: Is to combine public interest and private advantage! Truly a master stroke of morality, My Lord!

THE COUNT: You say that it's fear of young men that makes him lock his doors?

FIGARO: Yes, to everyone – without exception. If he could wall her up or brick her up he would do so.

THE COUNT: Ah! The Devil! That's not so good. Could you by any chance get access to the house?

FIGARO: Could I? In the first place the house I'm living in belongs to the worthy Doctor and he lodges me *gratis*.

THE COUNT: Ha! Ha!

FIGARO: And I in return promise him six gold pistoles a year – also *gratis*.

THE COUNT [*impatiently*]: You are his tenant?

FIGARO: And what's more his barber, his surgeon, his apothecary. There's never a scrape of a razor or probe of a lancet or a squirt of syringe in his household except at the hands of yours truly.

THE COUNT [*embracing him*]: Ah! Figaro! My friend! You shall be my guardian angel, my liberator, my guiding spirit.

FIGARO: Plague on it! How friendly people do become when they find they've a use for you. Talk about excitable fellows!

THE COUNT: Ah! Happy Figaro! You are going to see my Rosine! You'll actually see her. Think how lucky you are!

FIGARO: Oh, yes, that's how all lovers talk! Am *I* supposed to adore her as well? I only wish you could take my place.

THE COUNT: Oh, if only one could get past the guard!

FIGARO: That's just what I was thinking about.

THE COUNT: If only for a few hours. . . .

FIGARO: Give people problems of their own to think about and you prevent them from interfering with others.

THE COUNT: Yes, but what has that to do with it?

FIGARO [*pondering*]: I'm just wondering whether my knowledge of pharmacy wouldn't provide some means of . . .

THE COUNT: Villain!

FIGARO: I'm not going to hurt them, am I? They all need my ministrations. It's just a question of dosing them all at one and the same time.

THE COUNT: Surely the doctor would suspect something?

FIGARO: We must act so quickly that there'll be no time for suspicion to arise. I've got an idea: the Royal Infante's Regiment is coming to the town.

THE COUNT: The Colonel's a friend of mine.

FIGARO: Good. Present yourself at the Doctor's house in trooper's uniform with a billeting notice. He'll have to take you in, and you can leave the rest to me.

THE COUNT: Excellent!

FIGARO: It wouldn't be a bad thing if you pretended to be half-seas over. . . .

THE COUNT: What for?

FIGARO: And under a guise of being fuddled led him on a bit. . . .

THE COUNT: Why?

FIGARO: So that he wouldn't take umbrage and would think that you were more interested in sleep than in carrying on an intrigue under his roof.

THE COUNT: A very proper notion. But aren't you going to be there yourself?

FIGARO: Me? Oh, yes, of course, but we shall be pretty lucky if he doesn't guess who you are, even though he's never seen you before. Then how should we get you in afterwards?

THE COUNT: You are right there.

FIGARO: The fact is that you mayn't be able to act the part – it's difficult. A soldier – drunk . . .

THE COUNT: What do you take me for? [*Puts on a drunken manner.*] Is this the house of Doctor Bartholo, friend?

FIGARO: Not bad, I admit. A bit more unsteady on your pins though. [*In a more drunken tone*] Is thish the housh of . . .

THE COUNT: Oh, come! That's just vulgar drunkenness.

FIGARO: It's the right sort. It's the enjoyable sort.

THE COUNT: The door's opening.

FIGARO: Here he comes. We'll withdraw until he's gone.
    [*They conceal themselves.*]

BARTHOLO [*talking to someone inside as he comes out*]: I'll be back in a minute. Don't let anyone come in. What a fool I was to come down. I ought to have suspected something as soon as she asked me . . . and Bazile's not back yet. He was to make all arrangements for us to be married in secret tomorrow. Still no news at all! I must go see what's keeping him. [*Exit.*]

THE COUNT: What's that I heard? He's marrying Rosine in secret tomorrow!

FIGARO: Difficulties only add spice to the undertaking, My Lord!

THE COUNT: Who's this Bazile? What has he to do with the marriage?

FIGARO: He's a poor devil who teaches Bartholo's ward music. He's infatuated with his art, an accessory in knavery, needy, ready to grovel for half a crown. There'll be no difficulty in dealing with him, My Lord! [*Looking at the balcony*] There we go! Look!

THE COUNT: Who is it?

FIGARO: There, behind the lattice. Don't look now! Don't look!

THE COUNT: Why?

FIGARO: Didn't the note tell you to sing something or other? Go on. Sing as if you were singing . . . just for the sake of singing. There she is! There she is!

THE COUNT: Since I've aroused her interest without her knowing who I am, we'll keep to the assumed name of Lindor: I shall enjoy my triumph all the more. [*He opens the paper which Rosine threw down.*] But how am I to sing this? I can't make up the words. . . .

FIGARO: Anything that comes into your head will do, My Lord. When it comes to love-making it doesn't matter whether what one says makes sense or it doesn't. Here, take my guitar.

THE COUNT: But what do you expect me to do with it? I play so badly.

FIGARO: Surely there can't be anything a man like you can't make some attempt at! Go on! With the back of your hand. . . . So! *Plan, plan, plan,* you can't sing without a guitar in Seville . . . you would be found out and sent about your business in no time!

[FIGARO *keeps close to the wall under the balcony*.]

THE COUNT [*walking up and down, singing to his own accompaniment*]:

> Since you so wish, my name I will reveal
> Although unknown I would adore.
> Once known what can I hope for more?
> But still – my mistress' wish I must obey.

FIGARO [*whispering*]: Very good. Keep it up, My Lord.

THE COUNT [*as before*]:

I am Lindor, a name
As yet unknown to rank or fame.
Wealth too, alas, I cannot proffer
My love for you is all I have to offer.

FIGARO: Damn it! I couldn't do better myself, and I fancy myself at the game!

THE COUNT [*as before*]:

Tenderly each day I sing
From love for you I hope nothing
Save for a glimpse of those bright eyes
As you, my love, give ear unto my rhapsodies.

FIGARO: Goodness me! For that last bit I can only . . . [*Kisses the hem of his cloak.*]

THE COUNT: Figaro!

FIGARO: Excellency.

THE COUNT: Do you think she heard me?

ROSINE [*singing within the house*]:

All things assure me that I must
My heart to Lindor's care entrust.

[*The noise of a casement being slammed is heard.*]

FIGARO: Now do you think she heard you?

THE COUNT: She closed the window. Someone must have come into the room.

FIGARO: Ah! Poor little thing! How her voice trembled. She's taken a fancy to you all right, My Lord!

THE COUNT: She used the very method she herself suggested.

'All things assure me that I must
My heart to Lindor's care entrust.'

What grace! What intelligence!

FIGARO: What craft! What cunning love gives 'em!

THE COUNT: Do you think she'll consent to be mine, Figaro?

FIGARO: She'll jump from that balcony rather than fail you.

THE COUNT: Then it's settled. I'm Rosine's – for life!

FIGARO: You are forgetting, My Lord. She can't hear you now!

THE COUNT: Master Figaro. Just let me tell you this. *She is going to be my wife.* If you help me and conceal my identity . . . you understand . . . you know me sufficiently . . .

FIGARO: Yes, I agree. Come, Figaro, my lad, forward to fortune!

THE COUNT: Let us retire in case we arouse suspicion.

FIGARO [*vigorously*]: Look! I'm going in there – and with one stroke of my wand I'll lull vigilance to sleep, awake the transports of love, thwart the machinations of jealousy, confound base intrigue, and overcome every obstacle that confronts us. As for you, My Lord, to my house, in soldier's uniform with billeting notice in your hand and plenty of gold in your pockets.

THE COUNT: Who's the gold for?

FIGARO: Goodness me! Never mind who it's for! Gold is the sinews of intrigue!

THE COUNT: Don't worry, Figaro. I'll bring plenty.

FIGARO [*going*]: I'll rejoin you shortly.

THE COUNT: Figaro?

FIGARO: What is it?

THE COUNT: What about your guitar?

FIGARO: Fancy my forgetting my guitar! [*Going*] I must be demented!

THE COUNT: And your house? Where d'ye live, you blockhead?

FIGARO [*coming back*]: I really must be a bit touched. My shop is only a stone's throw away. Painted blue – leaded windows, barber's pole, and the sign '*Consilio Manuque*' – by Skill and Dexterity – and the name –

FIGARO, FIGARO, FIGARO!

[*Exit.*]

ACT TWO

SCENE: *Rosine's apartment, a casement window upstage – closed by a barred shutter.*

[ROSINE *is alone, a candlestick in her hand. She sits down at the table and begins to write.*]

ROSINE: Marceline is unwell: all the servants are busy and no one can see that I'm writing. I don't know whether walls have eyes – and ears, or whether my Argus-eyed keeper has some wicked fairy who keeps him informed of everything that happens, but I can't utter a word or move hand or foot without his guessing my intentions at once. . . . Ah, Lindor! [*Sealing the letter*] I'll seal it now though I don't know when or how I shall be able to get it into his hands. I saw him through the casement bars in conversation with Figaro the barber. *He's* a good fellow and has often shown his sympathy for me. If I could have a word with him for a moment . . .

[*Enter* FIGARO.]

ROSINE [*startled*]: Ah, Mr Figaro! I *am* pleased to see you.

FIGARO: I hope I find you well, Madam?

ROSINE: Not very well, Figaro. I'm dying of boredom.

FIGARO: I believe it. You'd need to be dull-witted to thrive on this sort of life.

ROSINE: Who were you having such a lively conversation with out there? Not that I was noticing particularly, but . . .

FIGARO: A young kinsman of mine. A most promising young man, clever, sensitive, talented, and quite attractive to look at.

ROSINE: Very nice, I must say! And his name?

FIGARO: Lindor. He hasn't any money – but he might have found himself a good position if he hadn't left Madrid in a hurry.

ROSINE [*indifferently*]: Oh, he'll find something yet, Figaro, he'll find something! A young man such as you've described can't fail to make a name for himself.

FIGARO [*aside*]: So far, so good! [*To Rosine*] Unfortunately he has one great defect which will always stand in the way of his getting on in the world.

ROSINE: A defect, Figaro? A defect? Are you sure?

FIGARO: He's in love.

ROSINE: In love! You call that a defect?

FIGARO: Of course – considering that he hasn't any money.

ROSINE: Oh, isn't fate unjust? And has he mentioned who it is . . . he's in love with? I'm always inquisitive . . .

FIGARO: You are the last person, Madam, to whom I would wish to make such a disclosure.

ROSINE [*quickly*]: But why, Mr Figaro? I'm very discreet and I'm very much interested in this young man of yours. Do tell me –

FIGARO [*looking slyly at her*]: Then think of the prettiest little creature imaginable, gentle, tender, charming, in fact quite irresistible. So light of foot, so trim of figure, such shapely arms, such rosy lips, such hands, such teeth, such eyes. . . .

ROSINE: And she's here in this town?

FIGARO: In this very quarter.

ROSINE: In this street perhaps?

FIGARO: Nearer than that. . . .

ROSINE: But how charming . . . for this young relation of yours. And the young lady is . . .

FIGARO: Didn't I mention her name?

ROSINE: It's the one thing you've forgotten, Mr Figaro. Do tell me at once. If a certain person were to come into the room I might never know.

FIGARO: And you really *must* know? Why then . . . the young lady is . . . the ward . . . of your guardian.

ROSINE: The ward of . . .?

FIGARO: Of Doctor Bartholo. Now you know!

ROSINE [*blushing*]: Ah, Figaro! I don't believe it. I just don't believe it.

FIGARO: He's only longing to come and convince you himself.

ROSINE: You frighten me, Figaro.

FIGARO: Frighten you! Fie! That's quite the wrong attitude. Once give way to fear of the consequences and you begin to experience them. Moreover, I've just got rid of your warders, till tomorrow at any rate.

ROSINE: If he loves me he could prove it by keeping absolutely tranquil and calm.

FIGARO: Ah, Madam! Did you ever know love and tranquillity go together? Youth is so unfortunate today – it's always faced with the same terrible choice: love without tranquillity or tranquillity without love.

ROSINE [*dropping her eyes*]: Tranquillity without love would seem . . .

FIGARO: Ah! Very sad, wouldn't it? In fact, love without tranquillity would seem to be . . . the better alternative and if I were a woman . . .

ROSINE [*with embarrassment*]: It's true that a young lady can't prevent a young man from esteeming her.

FIGARO: And my kinsman has the greatest possible esteem for you.

ROSINE: But if he should commit any imprudence, Mr Figaro, we should be lost.

FIGARO [*aside*]: We should indeed! [*To Rosine*] Perhaps if you were to send him a note – warning him particularly against it . . . a letter can do a great deal.

ROSINE [*handing him the letter she has just been writing*]: I have no
time to write this again, but when you give it him be sure
to say . . . [*She listens.*]

FIGARO: Nobody there.

ROSINE: . . . that what I'm doing is only in friendship.

FIGARO: That goes without saying. Good lord, yes! Love
would be a different thing altogether.

ROSINE: Only in friendship, you understand? Nothing more.
Yet I'm only afraid he may be put off by the difficulties . . .
and . . .

FIGARO: Like a will-o'-the-wisp, eh? But remember, Madam,
that the same wind which extinguishes a lamp will fan a fire
and that we men are like fires. Indeed, I may say that he's in
such a state that he's almost inflamed me with his passion –
and I'm only an onlooker.

ROSINE: Heavens! I hear my guardian! If he were to find you
here! Go through the music-room and down the stairs as
quietly as you can.

FIGARO: Don't worry. [*Aside – indicating the letter*] This will
have more effect than anything I say. [*He goes out.*]

ROSINE: I shan't have a moment of peace until he's safely
outside. I am so fond of dear Figaro. He *is* a nice man –
and so good to his relations. Ah! Here comes my tyrant.
I'll take up my work again.

[*She puts out the candle, sits down, and picks up her embroidery
frame.* BARTHOLO *enters in a rage.*]

BARTHOLO: Damnation! It's infuriating! That scoundrelly
thief of a Figaro! You can't leave the place for a moment
but when you get back . . . you can be certain that . . .

ROSINE: Has someone been annoying you, Sir?

BARTHOLO: It's that confounded barber. He's just put the
whole household out of action at one swoop. He's given
Wakeful a sleeping draught, Youthful a sneezing powder,
and he's bled Marceline in her big toe: even my mule – he's

put a poultice on the eyes of the poor blind creature! Because he owes me a hundred crowns he's trying to run up a bill for me! Ah! Let him pay what he owes! There's not a soul about downstairs. Anyone can come up here. It's as open as a barrack square.

ROSINE: But who can get in but you, Sir?

BARTHOLO: I'd rather be alarmed unnecessarily than not take every precaution. There are fellows up to tricks everywhere, the audacious scoundrels! Didn't some rascal nip off with your music only this morning while I was on my way down to get it? Oh! If only I . . .

ROSINE: You take a pleasure in exaggerating things. The wind may have taken it – or some passer-by.

BARTHOLO: Wind, eh? Some passer-by? There wasn't a breath of wind, Miss! Nor passer-by neither. Not a soul! When it comes to picking up paper that a young woman pretends to let fall by accident, it's someone posted there expressly for the purpose!

ROSINE: Pretends to let fall by accident, Sir?

BARTHOLO: Yes, Madam, *pretends*!

ROSINE [*aside*]: The cunning old wretch!

BARTHOLO: Yes, but it won't happen again. I'm going to fasten up this lattice.

ROSINE: Don't stop at that! Wall up the window at the same time! Prison or dungeon – it doesn't make much difference.

BARTHOLO: It wouldn't be a bad idea – those that give on to the street. I suppose that barber hasn't been here by any chance?

ROSINE: Oh! Are you worried about him too?

BARTHOLO: Every man Jack of them – they are all alike.

ROSINE: That's a nice answer, I must say!

BARTHOLO: Ay! Put your confidence in people and you'll soon have your women deceiving you, your best friends taking advantage of you, and your honest servants aiding and abetting.

ROSINE: What! Don't you even credit me with sufficient principle to resist the seductions of Mr Figaro?

BARTHOLO: Who the Devil can make any sense of women and their fancies? A lot I've seen of these virtuous principles!

ROSINE [*angrily*]: Well, Sir! If you think that any sort of man will please us, how does it come about that I find you so extremely *dis*pleasing?

BARTHOLO [*taken aback*]: Why? Why? Look here! You never replied to my question about the barber!

ROSINE [*beside herself*]: Very well, then. Yes, he has been here. I *have* seen him. I *have* talked to him. And I don't mind telling you that I found him most kind and helpful. And I hope you choke with your own bad temper! [*She goes out.*]

BARTHOLO [*alone*]: Oh, the infidels! Those dogs of servants! Youthful! Wakeful! Where's that confounded Wakeful?

WAKEFUL [*entering yawning, half asleep*]: Ah! Aaah! [*Yawns.*]

BARTHOLO: Where were you, you stupid fool, when that barber got in here?

WAKEFUL: Master, I was . . . aaah! [*Yawns.*]

BARTHOLO: Up to some sort of scoundrelism no doubt! Didn't you see him?

WAKEFUL: Of course I seen him! Didn't he find I was ill? He said I was and he must have been right, because I began to feel weak in every limb just with listening to him talking! Ah! Ah! Ah!

BARTHOLO [*imitating him*]: Just with listening to him talking! Where's that good-for-nothing Youthful? Giving the lad drugs without a prescription from me! There's some sort of rascality in it somewhere.

[*Enter* YOUTHFUL – *an old man leaning on his stick. He sneezes several times.*]

WAKEFUL [*yawning*]: Youthful?

BARTHOLO: Keep your sneezes for another time!

YOUTHFUL: That's more than fifty times . . . fifty times . . . a minute. [*Sneezes.*] I'm all to pieces.

BARTHOLO: Look! I asked you both if somebody had been in to see Rosine? Why didn't you tell me that this barber . . .

WAKEFUL [*yawning*]: Is Mr Figaro somebody? Aah! Cha!

BARTHOLO: I bet the cunning dog has an understanding with her.

YOUTHFUL: I ask you, Master, is it fair, is it right, is it just? [*Sneezes.*]

BARTHOLO: Just? What has justice to do with miserable wretches like you? I'm your master, and what I say must be right.

YOUTHFUL [*sneezing*]: But damme, if a thing's true . . .

BARTHOLO: If a thing's true! If I don't want a thing to be true I take jolly good care that it isn't true. If any sort of rabble are to be allowed to be in the right what's to become of order and discipline?

YOUTHFUL [*sneezing*]: I'd just as soon have my notice. It's a terrible job, this. It's a hell of a life!

WAKEFUL: Decent servants treated like dogs!

BARTHOLO: Out you go then, decent servants! [*Imitates them*] Ercha! Ercha! One sneezes in my face and the other yawns under my very nose!

YOUTHFUL: Ah, Master! I assure you if it weren't for the young lady there would be no staying here at all. [*Goes out sneezing.*]

BARTHOLO: What a state that Figaro has put 'em into! I see what it is. The good-for-nothing wanted to wipe off my hundred crowns without so much as opening his purse.

[*Enter* DON BAZILE. FIGARO, *hidden in the cabinet, peeps out and listens from time to time.*]

BARTHOLO: Ah! Don Bazile, you've come to give Rosine her lesson?

BAZILE: There's no particular hurry.

BARTHOLO: I called at your house, but I didn't find you at home.

BAZILE: I was out, on your business. There's some rather bad news.

BARTHOLO: For you?

BAZILE: No, for you. Count Almaviva's in town.

BARTHOLO: Don't talk so loudly. You mean the fellow who was looking all over Madrid for Rosine?

BAZILE: He has taken rooms in the Plaza Major and goes out every day in disguise.

BARTHOLO: That certainly means trouble for me. What's to be done?

BAZILE: If he were an ordinary person we could find some way of dealing with him.

BARTHOLO: Yes. Lie in wait in the dark and . . .

BAZILE: *Bone Deus*. Compromise ourselves? No! Start some nasty rumour – well and good! When it begins to get round, spread the scandal for all that it's worth – *concedo* – that I'd agree to.

BARTHOLO: That's a curious way of getting rid of a man!

BAZILE: Calumny, Sir. You don't realize its effectiveness. I've seen the best of men pretty near overwhelmed by it. Believe me there's no spiteful stupidity, no horror, no absurd story that one can't get the idle-minded folk of a great city to swallow if one goes the right way about it – and we have some experts here! First the merest whisper skimming the earth like a swallow before the storm – *pianissimo* – a murmur and it's away sowing the poisoned seed as it goes. Someone picks it up and – *piano piano* – insinuates it into your ear. The damage is done. It spawns, creeps, and crawls and spreads and multiplies and then –

rinforzando – from mouth to mouth it goes like the very
Devil. Suddenly, no one knows how, you see Calumny
raising its head hissing, puffing, and swelling before your
very eyes. It takes wing, extending its flight in ever-widen-
ing circles, swooping and swirling, drawing in a bit here
and a bit there, sweeping everything before it, and breaks
forth at last like a thunder clap to become, thanks be to
Heaven, the general cry, a public *crescendo*, a chorus universal of hate, rage, and condemnation. Who the deuce can
resist it?

BARTHOLO: What *is* this twaddle, Bazile? What have your
piano and *crescendo* and all that to do with me?

BAZILE: What have they to do with you? What's done everywhere to deal with an enemy we must do here and now to
keep yours at a distance.

BARTHOLO: Keep him at a distance? I mean to marry her
before she even knows the fellow exists.

BAZILE: In that case you haven't a minute to lose.

BARTHOLO: And whose fault is that? Haven't I put you in
charge of the arrangements?

BAZILE: Yes, but you've skimped the expenses! Things like
an unequal marriage, an iniquitous verdict, a miscarriage of
justice are dissonances within the ordered harmony of
things: they need to be resolved by the harmonizing influence of gold.

BARTHOLO [*giving him money*]: I suppose you must have it
your own way. But let us get on with it.

BAZILE: That's something like talking. Tomorrow everything shall be completed. You must make sure that no one
tips her a warning today.

BARTHOLO: Leave that to me. Will you be back here this
evening?

BAZILE: Don't count on it. Arrangements for the marriage
will keep me busy all day. Don't count on it.

BARTHOLO [*going with him to the door*]: Allow me.

BAZILE: Don't trouble, Doctor, don't trouble.

BARTHOLO: No trouble at all. I want to lock the street door when you have gone.

[*They go.* FIGARO *comes out of the closet.*]

FIGARO: O wise precaution! Lock the street door! And I'll go and *un*lock it for the Count as I go. What a scoundrel he is, this Bazile! Fortunately he's an even bigger fool. You need position in the world, family name, rank, standing in fact, to achieve anything effective by Calumny. A fellow like Bazile could lie to his heart's content – no one would believe him.

ROSINE [*running out*]: What! Are you still here, Figaro?

FIGARO: Very fortunately for you, Miss. Your guardian and your singing master thought they were alone. They have just been speaking their minds. . . .

ROSINE: And you have been listening, Figaro? But don't you know that's very wrong?

FIGARO: Listening? You *have* to if you want to know what's going on. Let me tell you that your guardian is getting ready to marry you tomorrow.

ROSINE: Oh, Heavens!

FIGARO: Don't worry. We'll keep him so busy he won't be able to give it a thought.

ROSINE: There he is – coming back. Go down by the little stair. You have frightened the life out of me.

[*Exit* FIGARO.

Enter BARTHOLO.]

ROSINE: Have you had a visitor, Sir?

BARTHOLO: Don Bazile. I was showing him to the door, and with good reason too! You would have preferred it to be Master Figaro, no doubt.

ROSINE: It's all the same to me, I assure you.

BARTHOLO: I would like to know what that barber was so anxious to tell you.

ROSINE: You really want to know? He came to report how Marceline was. She isn't too well from what he was telling me.

BARTHOLO: Came to report, did he? I wouldn't mind betting he was commissioned to deliver a letter to you.

ROSINE: And from whom, may I ask?

BARTHOLO: From whom? From somebody women never mention. How do I know? Perhaps a reply to the paper you dropped from the window.

ROSINE [aside]: He hasn't missed a thing! [To Bartholo] It would serve you right if it were!

BARTHOLO [looking at her hands]: That's what it is. You've been writing.

ROSINE [embarrassed]: It would be interesting to know how you propose to make me confess it.

BARTHOLO [taking her hand]: There's no necessity. You've ink stains on your fingers. Ah! Cunning Signora!

ROSINE [aside]: The wretch!

BARTHOLO [still holding her hand]: Women think they can safely do anything if they are alone.

ROSINE: Of course. A fine sort of proof that is! Let me go. You are twisting my arm. I burned myself when I was snuffing the candle. I have always heard you should put ink on a burn immediately, and that's what I did.

BARTHOLO: That was what you did, was it? Then we'll see if a second piece of evidence confirms the first one. I happen to know that there were six sheets of paper in this writing case. I count them every morning and I did so today.

ROSINE [aside]: Simpleton! The sixth . . .

BARTHOLO [counting]: Two, three, four, five . . . I can see the sixth isn't here.

ROSINE [lowering her eyes]: The sixth? . . . I used it to make a bag for the sweets I sent to Figaro's little girl.

BARTHOLO: Figaro's little girl? And the new pen nib, how does it come to be ink-stained? Did you use it to write the address of Figaro's little girl?

ROSINE [*aside*]: The man has an instinct for jealousy. [*To Bartholo*] I used it to retrace the flower pattern on the jacket I'm embroidering for you.

BARTHOLO: Very edifying indeed! But if you want people to believe you, my child, you shouldn't blush at each new shift to which you are driven for hiding the truth. You've not learned that yet.

ROSINE: Who wouldn't blush to see such horrid conclusions drawn from things done in all innocence?

BARTHOLO: Oh! Of course I was wrong! Burning one's finger, dipping it in ink, making sweet-bags for Figaro's little girl, tracing designs on my jacket, what could be more innocent? . . . What a pack of lies just to hide one single fact. *I was alone. Nobody could see me. I could lie to my heart's content.* But the stain is still there on the finger, the pen has been used, the sixth sheet is missing! One can't think of everything! What is certain, Signora, is that when I go out into the town I'll see that the door's double-locked on you!

[*Enter the* COUNT *in trooper's uniform, apparently half-seas over and singing* 'Let us awake her!'*]

BARTHOLO: What does this fellow want? A soldier! Go to your room, Signora.

THE COUNT [*singing – goes towards Rosine*]: Which of you ladies is Doctor Barordo? [*Whispers to Rosine*] I am Lindor.

BARTHOLO: Bartholo.

ROSINE [*aside*]: He spoke of Lindor!

THE COUNT: Balordo! Batorlo! Malodar! I don't care what it is. All I want to know is which of the two of you . . . [*To Rosine*] Take this letter.

BARTHOLO: Which of the two! You can see perfectly well it's

* A popular song of the period.

me. Which of the two! Go to your room, Rosine. The man appears to be drunk.

ROSINE: But, Sir, . . . you are alone. A woman sometimes has a restraining influence.

BARTHOLO: Go along. Go along. I'm not frightened of him. [*She goes.*]

THE COUNT: Oh! I knew you at once from your official description.

BARTHOLO [*to the Count who is putting the letter away*]: What is that you are hiding in your pocket?

THE COUNT: I'm hiding it in my pocket so that you shan't know what it is.

BARTHOLO: My official description? These fellows always think they are talking to soldiers.

THE COUNT: You don't think there's any difficulty in identifying you, do you? [*Sings*]

> Old and bald and palsied too
> Foxy-looking, cock-eyed, who
> Can it be, Doctor, but you?
> Bowlegged, stooping, pincer toes,
> That's how the description goes.
> Mumbling, grumbling,
> Weak and fumbling . . . *ad lib* . . .

BARTHOLO: Here! What does this mean? Have you come here to insult me? Get out! At once!

THE COUNT: Get out! Now, now! That's no way to talk. Can't you read, Doctor Bartholo?

BARTHOLO: Preposterous question!

THE COUNT: Don't let it worry you. Neither can I. Yet I'm just as good a doctor as you.

BARTHOLO: How do you make that out?

THE COUNT: Am I not the regimental horse doctor? That's why they billeted me on you – we are colleagues!

BARTHOLO: You have the audacity to compare a vet . . .

THE COUNT [*sings*]:
>   No, Doctor dear, we don't pretend
>   *Our* art can with yours contend.
>   Yours not only cures the cough
>   But the patient carries off. . . .

That's right, isn't it?

BARTHOLO: It ill becomes you – you ignorant bone-setter – to revile the first, foremost, and most beneficial of the sciences.

THE COUNT: Entirely beneficial – to those who practise it.

BARTHOLO: One on whose glory the sun never sets.

THE COUNT: Whose boss-shots the whole earth is insufficient to cover.

BARTHOLO: You oaf! It's obvious you aren't used to talking to anyone but horses.

THE COUNT: Talking to horses! Come, Doctor, from an intelligent man like you! Isn't it common knowledge that while the vet cures his patients without talking to them, the doctor talks to his without . . .

BARTHOLO: Without curing them, I suppose?

THE COUNT: You said it!

BARTHOLO: Who the Devil sent this confounded drunkard here?

THE COUNT: Now you are trying to flatter me.

BARTHOLO: Anyhow. What d'ye want? What did you come for?

THE COUNT [*pretending to be very annoyed*]: All right, then! He's getting annoyed is he! What do I want? Can't you see what I want?

ROSINE [*running into the room*]: Mr Soldier, please don't be angry. [*To Bartholo*] Talk to him gently, Sir. He's just talking nonsense.

THE COUNT: That's quite right. He's just talking nonsense, that fellow, but we are talking sense, we are! You are pretty, I'm polite, and that's all that matters. The truth is you are the only person in the house I want to have anything to do with.

ROSINE: And what can I do for you, Mr Soldier?

THE COUNT: A mere trifle, my dear. If what I'm saying isn't very clear . . .

ROSINE: I shall get the spirit of it.

THE COUNT [*showing her the letter*]: Never mind the spirit, stick to the *letter*. It's entirely a question of . . . but what I really mean to say is that you've got to put me up for the night.

BARTHOLO: That's all, is it!

THE COUNT: That's all. Nothing more. Read the nice little note that the billeting officer sent you.

BARTHOLO: Let me see.

[*The* COUNT *hides the letter and hands him another which* BARTHOLO *reads:*]

'Doctor Bartholo shall receive, lodge, shelter, and sleep . . .'

THE COUNT [*leaning*]: Sleep!

BARTHOLO: '. . . for one night only the aforementioned Lindor, otherwise known as the Scholar, trooper of the regiment of . . .'

ROSINE: 'Tis he! 'Tis he!

BARTHOLO [*sharply to Rosine*]: What's the matter with *you*?

THE COUNT: Well, am I wrong now, Doctor Barpolo?

BARTHOLO: One would think the fellow took a deliberate pleasure in finding every possible way of deforming my name. The Devil take you with your Barbolo and Barpolo! Go tell your impudent billeting officer that since I came back from Madrid I'm exempt from having soldiers billeted upon me.

THE COUNT [*aside*]: Oh Lord! That's an awkward one!

BARTHOLO: Ha! my friend, that's one in the eye for you! It even sobers you up a bit, but get out all the same.

THE COUNT [*aside*]: I thought I'd given myself away. [*To Bartholo*] Get out of it, eh? If you are exempt from billeting you aren't exempt from civility, or are you? Get out! Show me your certificate of exemption. I'll have a look at it even though I can't read it!

BARTHOLO: You won't get away with that! It's in my bureau. [*Goes to get it.*]

THE COUNT [*while* BARTHOLO *is busy*]: Ah! My charming Rosine!

ROSINE: Lindor! Can it really be you?

THE COUNT: Take this letter.

ROSINE: Be careful. He's watching us.

THE COUNT: Take out your handkerchief and I'll drop the letter. [*Goes towards her.*]

BARTHOLO: Go easy, soldier. I don't like folk getting too near my wife.

THE COUNT: *Is* she your wife?

BARTHOLO: What's that to you?

THE COUNT: I took you for her great-great-grandparent paternal, maternal, and sempiternal. There must be at least three generations between you.

BARTHOLO [*reading from a parchment*]: 'Upon report of good and faithful witnesses . . .'

THE COUNT [*knocking the parchment out of his hand*]: What's all this clap-trap to me . . . ?

BARTHOLO: Do you realize, soldier, that if I call my servants I can have you dealt with as you deserve here and now?

THE COUNT: A fight, eh? Willingly! Fighting's my job! [*Indicates his pistol.*] And here's the wherewithal for throwing the dust in their eyes. You've never seen a battle, Madam?

ROSINE: No, and I don't want to!

THE COUNT: There's no better fun than a battle. Imagine –

[*pushing the Doctor*] imagine the enemy on one side of the trench and our people on the other. [*Indicates letter to Rosine.*] Take out your handkerchief. [*Spits on the floor.*] That's the ditch, you see.

> [ROSINE *takes out her handkerchief. The* COUNT *drops the letter between them.*]

BARTHOLO [*stooping for it*]: Ha ha!

THE COUNT [*picking it up*]: Steady! Just when I was going to teach you my professional secrets. . . . A discreet young woman I must say? She lets a love-letter fall out of her pocket and . . .

BARTHOLO: Give it me.

THE COUNT: *Dulciter!* Gently, Papa! Everyone to his own business. Suppose a prescription for a purgative had fallen out of your pocket, now . . .

ROSINE: Ah! [*Puts out her hand.*] I know what it is Mr Soldier. [*Takes letter and puts it in her apron pocket.*]

BARTHOLO: Are you going or not?

THE COUNT: Right! I'm going. Good-bye, Doctor. No offence, eh? A little suggestion to you, my dear: pray that death may spare me for another campaign or two. I never felt that life was so dear to me.

BARTHOLO: Do be off. If I had any influence with death . . .

THE COUNT: If you had any influence with death? Aren't you a doctor? You do so much for death, how could it refuse you anything in return? [*Goes.*]

BARTHOLO: He's gone at last. [*Aside*] I must dissimulate.

ROSINE: You must agree that he's very lively. In spite of his being drunk, one could see that he was not wanting in intelligence or even a certain degree of breeding.

BARTHOLO: We are lucky to have got rid of him, my dear. And now wouldn't you like to read me the letter he left with you?

ROSINE: Which letter?

BARTHOLO: The one he handed to you under pretence of picking it up.

ROSINE: Oh, that! It's a letter from my cousin. It fell out of my pocket.

BARTHOLO: My impression was that he took it out of his.

ROSINE: I recognized it as mine.

BARTHOLO: Why not have a look at it?

ROSINE: I'm not sure what I did with it.

BARTHOLO [*pointing*]: You put it in there.

ROSINE: Oh, dear! How absent-minded!

BARTHOLO: Oh, of course! You'll see it's some nonsense or other.

ROSINE [*aside*]: Unless I can make him angry I shall have no excuse for refusing.

BARTHOLO: Come, hand it to me, my dear.

ROSINE: But why are you so insistent? Do you still not trust me?

BARTHOLO: But why shouldn't you show it me?

ROSINE: I tell you again, Sir, that this letter is the one from my cousin that you handed to me already opened yesterday. And while we are about it let me tell you that I very much resent such a liberty on your part.

BARTHOLO: I don't understand.

ROSINE: Do *I* examine your letters? Why should you presume to interfere with mine? If the motive is jealousy I consider it an insult; if it is a matter of assuming authority over me I find it still more intolerable.

BARTHOLO: Intolerable? How do you mean? You've never spoken to me like this before.

ROSINE: If I have restrained myself hitherto that gives you no right to insult me with impunity!

BARTHOLO: What insult are you referring to?

ROSINE: I mean it's an unheard of liberty to open other people's letters.

BARTHOLO: One's wife's?

ROSINE: I'm not your wife yet, but why subject a wife to an indignity you wouldn't show anyone else?

BARTHOLO: You are trying to involve me in argument and distract my attention from the letter. It undoubtedly comes from some lover. I insist upon seeing it!

ROSINE: You shan't see it. If you come near me I'll run out of the house and throw myself on the mercy of the first person I meet.

BARTHOLO: And a lot of notice he'd take of you.

ROSINE: That we shall see.

BARTHOLO: This isn't France where women are allowed to do as they like, so put that idea out of your head. I'll go and shut the door.

ROSINE [*as he is out of the room*]: Heavens! What am I to do? I must change it for my cousin's letter and let him have the pleasure of reading that. [*Changes the letters and allows her cousin's letter to protrude from her pocket a little.*]

BARTHOLO [*returning*]: Now I *am* going to see it!

ROSINE: By what right, if you please?

BARTHOLO: The right that is universally acknowledged – that of the stronger.

ROSINE: I'll die rather than give it up.

BARTHOLO [*stamping with rage*]: Now then, Miss! Now then!

ROSINE [*sinking into a chair and pretending to be ill*]: Ah! What an outrage!

BARTHOLO: Give me the letter or take the consequences.

ROSINE: Unhappy Rosine! [*Collapses.*]

BARTHOLO: What's wrong with you?

ROSINE: Oh! Hideous prospect!

BARTHOLO: Rosine!

ROSINE: I'm choking with rage.

BARTHOLO: She's ill.

ROSINE: I feel faint – I'm dying.

BARTHOLO [*taking her pulse – aside*]: Heavens! The letter. I'll read it without her knowing. [*He takes her pulse and tries to read the letter at the same time.*]

ROSINE [*still prostrate*]: Unfortunate that I am!

BARTHOLO [*aside, dropping her hand*]: How we long to learn what we most fear to know!

ROSINE: Poor Rosine!

BARTHOLO: It's the use of perfumes which produces these spasmodic affections. . . . [*Reads.*]

[ROSINE *takes a look at him out of the corner of her eye and resumes her position as before.*]

Heavens! It *is* her cousin's letter. Oh, cursèd mistrust! How can I propitiate her now? At least she shan't know that I read it. [*Pretends to hold her and slips the letter back in her pocket.*]

ROSINE [*taking a deep breath*]: Ah!

BARTHOLO: There, child, it's nothing. Just a touch of the vapours, that's all. Your pulse is as steady as can be. [*Goes to get a bottle from the side-table.*]

ROSINE [*aside*]: He's put it back. Excellent.

BARTHOLO: My dear Rosine, take a sip of this spirit.

ROSINE: I want nothing from you. Leave me!

BARTHOLO: I perhaps went too far in the matter of the letter.

ROSINE: You may well talk of the letter. It's your way of demanding things that is so revolting.

BARTHOLO [*on his knees*]: Forgive me. I realize I was wrong. You see me on my knees. All I ask is to be allowed to make amends.

ROSINE: Forgive you! And yet you still don't believe that the letter is from my cousin.

BARTHOLO: I am not asking to know who it comes from – from him or from anyone else.

ROSINE [*giving him the letter*]: You see. Behave reasonably to me and you can have anything you ask. Read it.

BARTHOLO: Such frankness would remove all suspicion even if I still had any.

ROSINE: Read it, then, Sir.

BARTHOLO [*stepping back*]: Heaven forbid that I should do such a thing!

ROSINE: I would much rather you read it.

BARTHOLO: Let me give you a mark of my confidence in return. I'm going up to see poor Marceline whom that Figaro has been bleeding – goodness knows why! Will you come too?

ROSINE: I'll come up in a minute.

BARTHOLO: Since peace is made, my dear, give me your hand on it. If only you could love me – Ah! How happy you would be!

ROSINE [*lowering her glance*]: If you knew how to please me – Ah! How I should love you.

BARTHOLO: I will please you. I will. And when I say it I mean it. [*He goes out.*]

ROSINE [*watching him go*]: Ah, Lindor! *He* says he will please me! I must read this letter which so nearly brought trouble upon me. [*Exclaiming as she reads*] Ha! I'm too late. He advises me to seek an occasion for a quarrel with my guardian. I had one and let it go. When I took the letter I felt myself blushing up to my eyes. Ah! How right my guardian was! – I am far from having that knowledge of the world which, I'm told, enables some women to maintain their composure in any circumstances. But a tyrant like this would contrive to make innocence itself become cunning.

ACT THREE

BARTHOLO [*alone and melancholy*]: What whims! What caprices! It seemed as if she was quite satisfied and now . . . What the Devil has put it into her head to refuse to have any more lessons from Don Bazile, that's what I would like to know! She knows he has something to do with the marriage. . . . [*Knock at the door.*] You can do anything in the world to please women and if you overlook one item . . . one single thing . . . [*Knock repeated.*] I must see who it is. [*Enter the* COUNT *as a young music master.*]

THE COUNT: May peace and happiness be upon this house.

BARTHOLO [*brusquely*]: Never was wish more timely! What do you want?

THE COUNT: Sir, my name is Alonzo, qualified master of . . .

BARTHOLO: I'm not needing a tutor.

THE COUNT: Pupil of Don Bazile, organist of the grand convent, who has the honour to teach singing to the young lady you . . .

BARTHOLO: Bazile! Organist! He has the honour! I know all about that.

THE COUNT [*aside*]: What a man! [*To Bartholo*] He's confined to his bed by a sudden indisposition.

BARTHOLO: Confined to bed? Bazile? He did right to let me know. I'll go see him at once.

THE COUNT [*aside*]: The Devil you will! [*To Bartholo*] When I said bed, I really meant bedroom. . . .

BARTHOLO: Let's hope it's not serious. Go ahead and I'll follow.

THE COUNT: Sir, I was charged to . . . can anyone hear us?

BARTHOLO [*aside*]: He's a rogue of some sort or other! [*To Count*] No, Master Mystery Monger, don't worry about being heard – speak out – if you can.

THE COUNT [*aside*]: Confound the old fogey! [*To Bartholo*] Don Bazile charged me to inform you . . .

BARTHOLO: Speak up! I'm deaf in one ear.

THE COUNT [*loudly*]: Willingly . . . to inform you that Count Almaviva who was lodging in the Plaza Major . . .

BARTHOLO: Not so loud. Not so loud.

THE COUNT [*louder than before*]: Left there this morning. As it was from me that he learned that Almaviva . . .

BARTHOLO: Please, not so loud.

THE COUNT [*as before*]: . . . that Almaviva was in town and as I had discovered that Signora Rosine had written to him . . .

BARTHOLO: She had written to him? My dear fellow, do speak more quietly, I implore you. Come, let us sit down and have a friendly chat together. You discovered, you say, that Rosine . . .

THE COUNT [*proudly*]: I certainly did! Bazile, alarmed on your behalf, asked me to come and show you her letter. Unfortunately you are taking things the wrong way. . . .

BARTHOLO: Heavens! I'm not taking anything the wrong way. But can't you possibly speak a bit more quietly?

THE COUNT: Didn't you say you were deaf in one ear?

BARTHOLO: I'm sorry, Signor Alonzo, if my manner seemed a little rude and suspicious, but I'm so surrounded by intrigue and intriguers . . . and then your appearance, your age, your manner . . . You must forgive me. Well now, you have the letter?

THE COUNT: That's more like the way to talk. But I'm concerned lest we should be overheard.

BARTHOLO: Why! Who could there be? The servants are all down and out! Rosine has shut herself up in a temper. The

Devil's in the house, but I'll go and make sure once again. [*He goes and carefully opens Rosine's door.*]

THE COUNT [*aside*]: I'm caught in my own trap. Better keep the letter for the present. I shall have to get out . . . better not have come . . . or should I show it him? If I could warn Rosine beforehand that would be a master stroke!

BARTHOLO [*tiptoeing back*]: She's sitting by the window with her back to the door reading her cousin's letter . . . the one I opened. Now let's have a look at hers.

THE COUNT [*giving him Rosine's letter*]: There you are. [*Aside*] It's *my* letter she's reading!

BARTHOLO [*reading*]: 'Since you have told me who and what you are. . . .' Ah! The sly wretch! And it's in her own handwriting.

THE COUNT [*in alarm*]: It's your turn to speak more quietly now!

BARTHOLO: How indebted I am to you, my dear fellow!

THE COUNT: When it's all over – if you still feel you owe me something – you will be able to . . . when Don Bazile has finished his present business with the lawyer –

BARTHOLO: You mean about my marriage?

THE COUNT: Of course. He told me to tell you that everything will be ready for tomorrow. Then if she resists . . .

BARTHOLO: She'll resist all right.

THE COUNT [*putting out his hand for the letter but* BARTHOLO *holds on to it*]: That's the point where I may be able to help you. We'll show her her own letter and, if necessary, [*mysteriously*] I'll go so far as to suggest to her that I got it from a woman the Count had given it to. You can imagine what sorrow and outraged pride may drive her to. . . .

BARTHOLO [*laughing*]: Calumny! My dear fellow, I can see now that you really do come from Bazile. But if it's not to seem like a put-up job wouldn't it be better that she should make your acquaintance beforehand?

THE COUNT [*repressing an exclamation of delight*]: That's just what Bazile thought. But how is it to be done? It's late and there's little time left now. . . .

BARTHOLO: I'll say you've come in his place. Couldn't you give her a lesson?

THE COUNT: I'll do whatever you like, but, you know, the singing-master story is a very old trick – it has a stagey look about it. Suppose she were to suspect?

BARTHOLO: There's no likelihood of that if *I* introduce you. Anyhow, you look more like a lover in disguise than the obliging friend of Bazile.

THE COUNT: Really? You think my manner might assist the deception?

BARTHOLO: I defy anyone to guess the truth. She's in a dreadful temper tonight, but she's only to see you and . . . her harpsichord is in this closet. Amuse yourself while you are waiting. I'll do all I can to bring her to reason.

THE COUNT: Be careful not to mention the letter.

BARTHOLO: Not until the vital moment! It would spoil the effect. You don't need to tell *me* things twice. No, I don't need to be told twice. [*He goes out.*]

THE COUNT [*alone*]: Saved! What a devilish awkward fellow to deal with! Figaro had him weighed up. The fact that I knew I was lying made me appear dull and stupid, but hasn't he sharp eyes! Upon my word, but for the sudden inspiration about the letter I should have been shown the door like a numbskull. Heavens! They are arguing. Suppose she continues to refuse to come out? I must listen! If she does refuse I lose all the advantage of my scheme. [*Listens at the door.*] Here she comes. I mustn't show myself yet. [*Goes into the closet.*]

ROSINE [*entering in simulated fury*]: It's no use your talking. I have made my decision. I want to hear no more talk about music.

BARTHOLO: Listen, child! It's Signor Alonzo, Don Bazile's friend and pupil – chosen by him to be one of our witnesses. . . . I assure you the music will have a soothing effect on you.

ROSINE: Well, you can get that out of your head. If I sing this evening I'll . . . Where is this fellow whom you are afraid to send packing? I'll give him his dismissal and Don Bazile as well and I won't waste any words on them either. [*Sees her lover.*] Ah!

BARTHOLO: What's the matter with you?

ROSINE [*her hands on her heart*]: Oh Heavens!

BARTHOLO: She's ill again. Signor Alonzo!

ROSINE: No, I'm not ill. It was in turning . . . Oh!

THE COUNT: You twisted your ankle?

ROSINE: Yes, I twisted my ankle. I hurt myself dreadfully.

THE COUNT: Yes, I saw that you did.

ROSINE [*looking at the Count*]: I'm quite overcome.

BARTHOLO: A chair! A chair! Why are there no chairs here! [*Goes to seek one.*]

THE COUNT: Ah, Rosine!

ROSINE: What imprudence!

THE COUNT: I have a thousand things I must tell you.

ROSINE: He'll never leave us alone.

THE COUNT: Figaro will come to our aid.

BARTHOLO [*bringing a chair*]: There, dearie, sit down. It doesn't look as if she'll be having her lesson this evening, young man. It will have to be another day. Good-bye.

ROSINE [*to the Count*]: No, wait a while. The pain is passing off a little. [*To Bartholo*] I feel I perhaps did you an injustice, Sir. Let me follow your example and make prompt amends. . . .

BARTHOLO: Ah! There's a good little woman, but after a shock like that I wouldn't have you try to do anything. Good-bye, young man. Good-bye!

ROSINE [*to the Count*]: A moment, please. [*To Bartholo*] I shan't believe that you want to please me if you prevent me from giving proof of my contrition by having my lesson.

THE COUNT [*to Bartholo*]: If you take my advice you'll let her have her own way.

BARTHOLO: Well then, my love, that's all right. So far from not wanting to please you I'll stay here while you have your lesson.

ROSINE: Oh, no, Sir! I know you aren't interested in music.

BARTHOLO: I assure you that I shall take the greatest possible interest in it this evening.

ROSINE [*aside to the Count*]: I'm in despair!

THE COUNT [*taking up a sheet of music*]: Is this what you would like to sing, Madam?

ROSINE: Yes. It's a charming passage from *The Futile Precaution.*

BARTHOLO: Still harping on your *Futile Precaution!*

THE COUNT: It's the very latest thing. It gives a kind of impression of spring and it's in a very lively style. If the young lady cared to try it . . .

ROSINE: With pleasure. An impression of spring would be delightful. Spring is nature's own season of youthfulness. It seems as if with the passing of winter the heart acquires a greater sensibility – as a captive long imprisoned and given an offer of freedom savours to the full the joys of liberation.

BARTHOLO [*to the Count*]: Her head's always full of these romantic ideas.

THE COUNT [*whispers to Bartholo*]: Don't you see the point?

BARTHOLO: Good Lord! [*He sits in the chair which Rosine has left.*]

ROSINE [*sings*]:

> When spring returns again
> Cupid resumes his reign.

All life pervading,
All things invading,
Flowers and lovers' hearts
Spring new warmth imparts.

From fold and grange
The flocks do range.
Young lambs abound
With their cries the hills resound.

Love doth resume its reign
For spring is come again.
Lindor can think of naught
Save what in him hath wrought
Love for his shepherdess
Wherein lies her happiness.

[BARTHOLO *dozes off. The* COUNT *takes Rosine's hand and covers it with kisses.* ROSINE'S *emotion causes her voice to falter and stops her song in mid-phrase. The orchestra stops also. The silence wakes* BARTHOLO, *whereon the* COUNT *resumes his position.* ROSINE *continues her song and* BARTHOLO *dozes off again – and so on.*]

THE COUNT: It certainly is a very charming little piece, and the young lady sings it very well indeed.

ROSINE: You flatter me. The credit lies entirely with the teacher.

BARTHOLO [*yawning*]: I think I must have dozed off during this charming little piece. I have my patients . . . I'm here and there and everywhere till I can hardly stand, and as soon as I sit down my poor feet . . . [*Gets up and pushes the chair away.*]

ROSINE [*aside to the Count*]: Figaro doesn't come.

THE COUNT: We must play for time.

BARTHOLO: I've already asked Bazile, young man, whether

she can't be given something a bit more lively than these
arias which go up up up and then down down down and
up up up ... dismal as a funeral to me they sound. What
about some of the little tunes they sang when I was young
... anybody could get hold of them without any trouble. I
used to know one, for example –

[*During the introduction he scratches his head to recall the words,
snaps his fingers as he sings, and bends and sways his knees in
time with the song as old men do.*
Sings]

> Wilt thou have me
> Rosinette?
> A prince of husbands
> You would get ...

[*Laughingly to the Count*] It's Fanchonette in the song, but I
sing Rosinette for fun and to make it fit in with us. Ha,
ha! Good, eh?

THE COUNT [*laughing*]: Yes, very good!

[*Enter* FIGARO *unobserved upstage.*]

BARTHOLO:

> Wilt thou have me
> Rosinette?
> A prince of husbands
> You would get.
> 'Tis true I am no beauty
> But I know a husband's duty
> And this much I can say –
> And this much I can say
> Though I may not look much catch by day
> In the dark all cats are grey!

[*He repeats from* 'This much I can say –' *dancing in time
with his singing.* FIGARO, *upstage, imitates him unseen.*]

BARTHOLO [*perceiving Figaro*]: Ah! Come in, Master Barber.
Come right in. You are a fine fellow, I must say!

FIGARO: That's what my mother used to say, but I've gone off a bit since those days. [*Aside to the Count*] Bravo, My Lord!

[*Throughout this scene the* COUNT *endeavours to speak to Rosine, but the guardian's watchful eye prevents it. The by-play goes on throughout the ensuing* BARTHOLO—FIGARO *dialogue.*]

BARTHOLO: Have you come to purge, bleed, and drug the whole house into bed again?

FIGARO: We don't have a celebration every day, Sir, but apart from my daily attentions you will have perceived that when need arises my zeal doesn't wait for instruction. . . .

BARTHOLO: You and your zeal! What are you going to say to the unfortunate fellow you've set yawning and dozing and to the other who's sneezing his head off? What are you going to say to them?

FIGARO: What am I going to say to them?

BARTHOLO: Yes.

FIGARO: I'll say . . . Lord, yes! I shall say to the sneezer, 'God preserve you!' And to the sleeper, 'Away to your bed!' And for that I shall charge you nothing, Sir!

BARTHOLO: I should think not. But you'd charge for your bleedings and purgings and drugs if I would let you. I suppose it was your zeal that made you blindfold my mule? Will your poultice give it its sight back I want to know?

FIGARO: If it doesn't give it its sight back at any rate it won't be what stops it from seeing!

BARTHOLO: Don't let me catch you putting that on the bill. I won't have that sort of nonsense.

FIGARO: Upon my word, Sir, mankind has no choice between one sort of folly and another, so where I can't have the profit at least let me have the pleasure. Here's to a life of mirth and jollity, say I! Who knows whether the world will last another three weeks?

BARTHOLO: You would do much better, Master Philosopher,

to pay me my hundred crowns and the interest you owe me without any more shilly-shallying, I warn you.

FIGARO: Do you doubt my honesty, Sir? Your hundred crowns! I would rather owe you them for a lifetime than deny you them for a single moment.

BARTHOLO: Yes! And now perhaps you will tell me how your little girl enjoyed the sweets you took her.

FIGARO: What sweets? What are you talking about?

BARTHOLO: The sweets you took this morning in the bag made from writing paper.

FIGARO: The Devil take me if I understand a word. . . .

ROSINE [*intervening*]: I hope you said they were from me as I asked you, Mr Figaro. . . .

FIGARO: Oh, you mean the sweets *this morning*! I'm stupid. I had forgotten all about them. Oh, yes, they were excellent, Madam, splendid!

BARTHOLO: Excellent! Splendid! That's better, Master Barber! Cover up your mistakes. It's a pretty sort of business, I must say!

FIGARO: What's the trouble, Sir?

BARTHOLO: You'll get yourself a fine reputation.

FIGARO: I'll try not to let it down, Sir.

BARTHOLO: You won't let *her* down, you mean.

FIGARO: Have it which way you please, Sir.

BARTHOLO: You are very hoity-toity, my good fellow, but let me warn you that when I'm involved with a knave I face him out to the end.

FIGARO [*turning his back*]: That's where we differ, Sir. I always give way to him.

BARTHOLO: Hey! What's that he said, young man?

FIGARO: The fact is, you think you have some village barber to deal with, a fellow with no ideas beyond his own trade. Let me tell you, Sir, that I have lived by my pen in Madrid and but for the envy of . . .

BARTHOLO: Then why didn't you stop there instead of coming here and changing professions!

FIGARO: A man must live as he can. Put yourself in my place.

BARTHOLO: Put myself in your place! I should talk nonsense then!

FIGARO: You aren't doing too badly now. I call on your colleague there who's day-dreaming to testify.

THE COUNT: I am not the gentleman's colleague.

FIGARO: No? Seeing you here in consultation I thought you were on the same job.

BARTHOLO [angrily]: Look here! What did you come for? Is there another letter to be handed to her? Speak up. Are you trying to get me out of here?

FIGARO: How you do go on at folks! I came in to shave you. That's all. Is it your day or isn't it?

BARTHOLO: You can come back again later.

FIGARO: Come back! And I with the whole garrison to physic tomorrow morning. I got the contract through influence, so you can guess whether I have any time to spare. Will you go into your own room, Sir?

BARTHOLO: No, I shall not go into my own room! What's to prevent your shaving me here?

ROSINE [scornfully]: You are polite! Why not in my bedroom?

BARTHOLO: Now you are getting annoyed. Forgive me, my child, you are going to finish your lesson, and I don't want to miss the pleasure of hearing it. Not a minute of it.

FIGARO [aside]: We shan't get him out of here. [Calling] Wakeful! Youthful! Basin, water, bring everything the master needs.

BARTHOLO: That's right! Call them! Worn out and weary, aching all over from your ministrations. Can't you leave them to sleep?

FIGARO: All right. I'll go and find what I need. Is it in your bedroom? [*To the Count in a whisper*] I am determined to get him out.

BARTHOLO [*fingering his key-ring*]: No, no! I'll go myself. [*Whispers to the Count as he goes*] Keep an eye on them.

FIGARO: Ah! To think what we missed! He was going to give me his keys. Was the key of the lattice there?

ROSINE: It's the new one. . . .

BARTHOLO [*coming back*]: I can't think what I'm doing to leave that accursed barber here. [*To Figaro*] Here. [*Hands him the keys.*] In my room, under the desk, but don't go touching anything.

FIGARO: Confound you! It would serve you right if I did, suspicious old thing that you are! [*Aside as he goes*] See how Heaven defends the righteous!

BARTHOLO [*to the Count*]: He's the joker who took the letter to the Count.

THE COUNT [*whispering*]: He has the look of a rogue to me.

BARTHOLO: He'll not catch me out again though.

THE COUNT: I think in that respect the worst is over.

BARTHOLO: All things considered, I thought it wiser to send him to my room rather than leave him here with her.

THE COUNT: They couldn't have said anything without my hearing.

ROSINE: Don't you think it rather rude to keep on whispering like this, gentlemen? What about my lesson?

[*Noise of crockery overturned off-stage.*]

BARTHOLO: Whatever's that? It's that dreadful barber letting everything fall down the stairs – all the best things I possess. [*He rushes out.*]

THE COUNT: We must use the moment Figaro's cleverness has given us. I implore you to accord me an interview this evening. I must save you from the bondage into which you are about to fall.

ROSINE: Ah, Lindor!

THE COUNT: I can climb to your balcony. As for the letter which I received from you this morning I found I had to . . .

[BARTHOLO *returns*.]

BARTHOLO: I wasn't mistaken. Everything broken – smashed to smithereens.

FIGARO: You see now what comes of so much hurry. I couldn't see a thing on the stairs. [*Shows the Count the key*.] Coming up the steps I got caught on a key.

BARTHOLO: You should look what you are doing. Caught on a key! You *are* a clever fellow, I must say.

FIGARO: My goodness, you find a cleverer!

[*Enter* BAZILE.]

ROSINE [*aside – in alarm*]: Don Bazile!

THE COUNT [*aside*]: Good Heavens!

FIGARO [*aside*]: Oh, the Devil!

BARTHOLO [*going up to him*]: Ah, Bazile, my dear friend, how good to see you better again. You *are* better, aren't you? No after-effects? Signor Alonzo really made me quite alarmed about you. I would have set off to see you at once if he hadn't restrained me.

BAZILE [*puzzled*]: Signor Alonzo?

FIGARO [*stamping his foot*]: Look! Am I to be held up again? Two hours over one miserable beard . . . a bitch of a trade, this.

BAZILE [*looking at them*]: Would you be so kind as to tell me, gentlemen . . .

FIGARO: You can talk to him when I have gone.

BAZILE: But mustn't I really . . .

THE COUNT: You really must shut up, Bazile! Do you think you can tell the gentleman anything he doesn't know already? I told him that you had arranged for me to come and give the music lesson in your place.

BAZILE [*more surprised than ever*]: The music lesson?...
Alonzo?

ROSINE [*aside to Bazile*]: Oh, do be quiet!

BAZILE: She as well?

THE COUNT [*whispering to Bartholo*]: Whisper to him what we
have arranged.

BARTHOLO [*aside to Bazile*]: Don't contradict us, Bazile. If
you say he's not your assistant you'll spoil everything.

BAZILE: Ah!

BARTHOLO: There's no doubt, Bazile, that your assistant
really is a very talented fellow.

BAZILE [*stupefied*]: My assistant! [*Whispering*] I came to tell
you that the Count has left his lodging.

BARTHOLO: I know. Be quiet.

BAZILE [*in a whisper*]: Who told you?

BARTHOLO [*whispering*]: *He* did of course.

THE COUNT [*in a whisper*]: Of course I did. Now listen.

ROSINE [*whispering to Bazile*]: Can you really not keep quiet?

FIGARO [*whispering to Bazile*]: You great oaf! Are you
deaf!

BAZILE [*aside*]: Who the Devil are we supposed to be deceiving? Everybody's in the secret.

BARTHOLO [*to Bazile*]: Well now, Bazile, what about the
lawyer?

FIGARO: You've all the evening to talk about your lawyer.

BARTHOLO: One word. Are you satisfied with the lawyer?

BAZILE [*alarmed*]: With the lawyer?

THE COUNT [*smiling*]: Haven't you seen the lawyer?

BAZILE [*impatient*]: No, I haven't seen any lawyer!

THE COUNT [*aside to Bartholo*]: Do you want him explaining
it all in front of her? Send him away.

BARTHOLO [*whispers to the Count*]: You are right. [*To Bazile*]
How did you come to be taken ill so suddenly?

BAZILE [*furious*]: I don't understand you.

THE COUNT [*slipping a purse into his hand*]: The gentleman wants to know what you are doing here at all in the state you are in.

FIGARO: He's as pale as death!

BAZILE: Ah, now I understand.

THE COUNT: Go straight to bed, my dear Bazile. You are not well. You are frightening us to death. Go to bed.

FIGARO: His face is all haggard. Go to bed!

BARTHOLO: Upon my word! One can diagnose fever a mile off! Go to bed!

ROSINE: Why ever did you come out? They say it's infectious. Go to bed!

BAZILE [*more astonished than ever*]: I'm to go to bed?

ALL: Of course. Go to bed.

BAZILE [*looking from one to another*]: Well then, gentlemen, I think I *had* better retire. I don't think I *am* quite myself.

BARTHOLO: Tomorrow then, if you are better.

THE COUNT: I'll be with you first thing.

FIGARO: Take my advice. Keep warm in bed.

ROSINE: Good night, Don Bazile.

BAZILE [*aside*]: Devil take me if I understand a word of it! If it weren't for the purse . . .

ALL: Good night, Bazile.

BAZILE: Very well, then, good night!
   [*They all laugh as they see him to the door.*]

BARTHOLO [*in a serious tone*]: The fellow really isn't at all well.

ROSINE: He has a wild look in his eye.

THE COUNT: He must have picked up a chill.

FIGARO: Did you notice how he talked to himself? It's as well it isn't one of us. [*To Bartholo*] Well, are you ready now?
   [*He puts the chair a long way from the Count and offers Bartholo the towel.*]

THE COUNT: Before we finish, Madam, I must just tell you

one important thing about the art which I have the honour to be teaching you. [*Goes up to her and whispers in her ear.*]

BARTHOLO [*to Figaro*]: Hey! It seems as if you are deliberately trying to keep in front of me so that I can't see . . .

THE COUNT [*whispers to Rosine*]: We have the key to the lattice. We'll be here at midnight!

FIGARO [*putting the towel round Bartholo*]: What is there to see? If it were a dancing lesson one could understand your wanting to watch, but singing . . . Ah!

BARTHOLO: What is it?

FIGARO: Something in my eye.

BARTHOLO: Don't rub it.

FIGARO: It's the left one. Do you mind looking into it for me?

[BARTHOLO *takes Figaro's head, looks at it, pushes him violently away, and steals across to listen to the conversation.*]

THE COUNT [*whispering*]: As for your letter . . . I was unable to remain here earlier and . . .

FIGARO [*warning them*]: Hem! Hem!

THE COUNT: In despair at finding my disguise was of no avail . . .

BARTHOLO [*passing between them*]: Your disguise was of no avail!

ROSINE [*alarmed*]: Ah!

BARTHOLO: Very well, Miss. Don't disturb yourself. What! Under my very eyes, in my presence – you have the audacity to put such an outrage upon me.

THE COUNT: What's the matter, Sir?

BARTHOLO: Perfidious Alonzo!

THE COUNT: Signor Bartholo! If you often have the sort of hallucinations I have just had the misfortune to witness I don't wonder at the lady's reluctance to become your wife.

ROSINE: His wife! Me! Spend all my days with a jealous old

man who can offer a young girl nothing but a life of horrible slavery!

BARTHOLO: What's this I hear?

ROSINE: I don't mind who hears. I will give my heart and my hand to the man who will snatch me from this terrible prison in which both my wealth and my person are illegally detained. [*She goes out.*]

BARTHOLO: I'm choking with rage.

THE COUNT: It is indeed difficult, Signor, for a young woman to . . .

FIGARO: Yes . . . a young woman and old age . . . that's what brings trouble on an old man's head.

BARTHOLO: What! When I catch them in the very act! Accursed barber! It makes me want to . . .

FIGARO: I'm going. He's mad!

THE COUNT: Me too! Upon my word, he *is* mad!

FIGARO: He's mad! Mad. Mad. Mad!
        [*They go.*]

BARTHOLO [*running after them*]: Mad, am I? Infamous scoundrels! Devil's emissaries come here to do his foul work. May he carry you off, every one of you! I'm mad! I saw them as plain as I see this desk. To brazen it out in front of me like that. Ah! Bazile's the only person who can make sense of this for me. I must go and find him. . . . Hello, somebody! . . . Ah, I forgot, there *is* nobody! . . . A neighbour, a passer-by, never mind who it is! It's enough to drive anyone mad! [*Repeats.*]

*

During the Interval the theatre darkens and the noise of a storm is heard. The orchestra plays the fifth piece of the music for The Barber.

ACT FOUR

[*The stage is in darkness.* BARTHOLO *and* DON BAZILE *discovered.* BAZILE *carries a paper lantern.*]

BARTHOLO: What? You don't know him? How can you say such a thing, Bazile?

BAZILE: If you asked me a hundred times I should still make the same answer. If he gave you Rosine's letter then he must beyond question be one of the Count's emissaries, but from the size of his tip he could well be the Count himself.

BARTHOLO: How could he be? But, by the way – talking of the tip – why did you accept it?

BAZILE: You seemed to be all friends together. I knew nothing about what was going on. In a case where it's difficult to make up one's mind a purse of gold always seems to me to be a conclusive argument. Then again, as the proverb says, Easy come –

BARTHOLO: I understand ... [*Holds out his hand.*] ... Easy go.

BAZILE: No – Easy kept!

BARTHOLO [*surprised*]: Oh!

BAZILE: I have arranged quite a number of little variations on well-known proverbs. But, to come to the point, what are you waiting for?

BARTHOLO: If you were in my place, Bazile, wouldn't you go to any lengths to possess her?

BAZILE: Upon my word, Doctor, I would *not*. With any sort of property it isn't possession that matters, it's the enjoyment of it that gives satisfaction. In my opinion marrying a woman who doesn't love you is running the risk of ...

BARTHOLO: Unfortunate consequences, you think, eh?

BAZILE: Well, well, you know – one sees it often enough nowadays. . . . I wouldn't marry her against her will.

BARTHOLO: Thank ye kindly, Bazile. Better she should weep at having *me* than that I should suffer by not having *her*.

BAZILE: It's a life-and-death matter, is it? Then marry her, Doctor, marry her by all means.

BARTHOLO: I will! This very night, too.

BAZILE: Good-bye then and remember when you are telling your ward about these chaps make them black as hell.

BARTHOLO: Right you are!

BAZILE: Calumny, Doctor, calumny! That's what it always comes to in the end.

BARTHOLO: Here's Rosine's letter that this fellow Alonzo brought me. He showed me how to make use of it without meaning to.

BAZILE: Good-bye. We shall all be here at four o'clock.

BARTHOLO: Why not earlier?

BAZILE: Impossible. The notary is already booked.

BARTHOLO: For a marriage?

BAZILE: Yes, at the house of Figaro the barber. His niece is going to be married.

BARTHOLO: His niece? He hasn't one!

BAZILE: That's what they told the notary.

BARTHOLO: The scoundrel's in the plot. The devil!

BAZILE: You don't think . . .?

BARTHOLO: Upon my word, they're a cunning lot! Look, friend, I'm not happy about this . . . go back to the notary's house and bring him here right away. . . .

BAZILE: It's raining. The very devil of a night, but nothing shall prevent my doing what you want. What are you doing now?

BARTHOLO: Seeing you to the door. Don't you know that

Figaro has put all my servants out of action? I'm alone in the house.

BAZILE: I have my lantern.

BARTHOLO: Look, Bazile. Here's my master key. I'll wait for you. I'll stay up come what may – apart from you and the notary not a soul shall come in here tonight.

[*They go out.* ROSINE *comes out of her bedroom.*]

ROSINE: I thought I heard someone talking. It has struck midnight and Lindor hasn't come. This weather was favourable to his plan. He was certain of meeting no one. Ah, Lindor! If you have deceived me ... what's that I hear? Heavens! It's my guardian. I must go in.

[*Re-enter* BARTHOLO.]

BARTHOLO [*holding light*]: Ah, Rosine, since you haven't yet retired to your room ...

ROSINE: I was just going to bed.

BARTHOLO: You won't sleep this wild night. I have some things I particularly want to tell you.

ROSINE: What do you want with me, Sir? Isn't it enough that I should be tormented by day?

BARTHOLO: Listen to me, Rosine.

ROSINE: Tomorrow.

BARTHOLO: A moment, please.

ROSINE [*aside*]: If only he would come!

BARTHOLO [*showing her the letter*]: Do you recognize this letter?

ROSINE [*recognizing it*]: Great Heavens!

BARTHOLO: I have no intention of reproaching you, Rosine. It is easy to make mistakes at your age. I am your friend. Listen to me.

ROSINE: I can bear no more.

BARTHOLO: This letter that you wrote to Count Almaviva ...

ROSINE: Count Almaviva!

BARTHOLO: You see what a monster the Count is. No sooner had he received the letter than he used it as evidence of his triumph. I got it from a woman he gave it to.

ROSINE: Count Almaviva!

BARTHOLO: You find it difficult to persuade yourself of such a horrible thing. Inexperience makes your sex credulous and confiding, Rosine, but you see now what a trap you have been led into. This woman told me the whole story – apparently with a view to getting rid of a dangerous rival. I shudder to think of it! A most horrible conspiracy between Almaviva, Figaro, and this supposed pupil of Don Bazile – Alonzo! That isn't his real name. He's no more than the vile instrument of the Count. This conspiracy was leading you into the abyss from which there could have been no rescuing you. . . .

ROSINE [overwhelmed]: Horrible! Lindor! What ... the young man who . . .

BARTHOLO [aside]: Ah! Lindor, is it?

ROSINE: To act for Count Almaviva – for another . . .

BARTHOLO: That's what I was told when I was given the letter.

ROSINE: Ah! What a shameful thing to do! He shall be punished! Sir, you wished to marry me?

BARTHOLO: You know the strength of my feelings.

ROSINE: If you are still of the same mind, I am yours.

BARTHOLO: Good! The notary shall come this very night.

ROSINE: That is not all. Oh, Heavens! Am I sufficiently humiliated? I must tell you that ... that perfidious wretch will shortly be here – he intends to get in by this lattice with the key which they have contrived to deprive you of.

BARTHOLO [looking at his key-ring]: Ah! The scoundrels! My child! I won't leave you for a moment.

ROSINE [alarmed]: But supposing they were armed?

BARTHOLO: True. I should lose my revenge. Go up to Marceline's room and lock yourself in. I must go and seek assistance and lie in wait for them near the house. If we can arrest them as thieves we shall have the pleasure of being avenged and delivered from them at one stroke. My love will be your recompense. . . .

ROSINE [*in despair*]: Only forget my error. [*Aside*] Ah! I'm sufficiently punished!

BARTHOLO [*going*]: I'll go prepare an ambush for them. I have her after all! [*Goes out.*]

ROSINE [*alone*]: *His* love as my recompense! Unhappy girl that I am! [*She weeps.*] What can I do? He will be coming. I'll remain here and keep up the pretence with him so that I can see him for a moment in all his wickedness. The baseness of his behaviour will preserve me from . . . and how I shall need it! Such nobility of countenance, such gentleness of manner, so tender a voice . . . to be no more than the vile instrument of a seducer!

[*She runs out.* FIGARO *in a cloak appears at the window.*]

FIGARO [*talking to someone outside*]: Somebody ran out of the room. Shall I go in?

THE COUNT [*without*]: A man?

FIGARO: No.

THE COUNT: Then it's Rosine. Your horrible appearance has frightened her.

FIGARO [*jumping down into the room*]: Upon my word, I believe it. Here we are at last in spite of rain, thunder, and lightning.

THE COUNT [*wrapped in a long cloak*]: Give me a hand. [*Jumps down.*] Victory is ours.

FIGARO [*throwing off his cloak*]: And we are wet to the skin! Charming weather to be out in search of adventure! How does the night suit you, My Lord?

THE COUNT: Splendid for a lover!

FIGARO: And for his assistant? Suppose someone were to surprise us here?

THE COUNT: Aren't you with *me*? I have something quite different to worry about. How am I to bring her to leave the Doctor's house here and now?

FIGARO: You have three all-powerful passions on your side. Love, hate, and fear.

THE COUNT [*looking into the darkness*]: How to break it to her that the notary is at your house waiting to unite us? She may well think my plans go too far. She may think me presumptuous.

FIGARO: If she says you presume too far reproach her with her cruelty. Women like being told they are cruel. Then, if her love proves to be all you wish, you reveal who you are. She won't have any more doubts about your sincerity then.

[*Enter* ROSINE. FIGARO *lights the candles.*]

THE COUNT: There she is. . . . Ah! My lovely Rosine!

ROSINE [*in a formal tone*]: I was beginning to think, Sir, that you were not coming.

THE COUNT: Charming anxiety! Madam, I ought not to take advantage of circumstances to propose that you should share the lot of a man without fortune, but whatever refuge you may choose I swear on my honour . . .

ROSINE: Sir, if the gift of my hand had not had to follow immediately on that of my heart you would not be here. Let necessity be your justification for any irregularity there may be in this meeting.

THE COUNT: But Rosine, to become the companion of a luckless fellow without birth or fortune . . .

ROSINE: Birth and fortune! Let us put aside such fortuitous accidents. If you assure me that your intentions are pure . . .

THE COUNT [*on his knees*]: Rosine! I adore you!

ROSINE [*indignantly*]: Stop! Miserable man! You dare to profane. . . . You adore me! . . . Adore me! . . . Go! You no longer have any influence over me. It only needed that word to make me detest you. But before I leave you to your own remorse [*weeping*] learn that I did love you, that all my happiness lay in sharing your unhappy lot . . . wretched Lindor! I was about to give up everything to go with you. But your own wickedness in taking advantage of my tenderness for you and the unworthy purposes of this horrible Almaviva to whom you betrayed me have put into my hands this proof of my folly. Do you recognize this letter?

THE COUNT: Your guardian handed it to you?

ROSINE [*proudly*]: Yes, and I thank him for doing so.

THE COUNT: Heavens! What happiness for me! He had it from my own hands. In my embarrassment last evening I used it as a means of gaining his confidence, and I never found an opportunity of warning you. Ah! Rosine! So it is true then that you love me.

FIGARO: My Lord, you were seeking . . . a woman who would love you for yourself alone!

ROSINE: What does he say? 'My Lord!'

THE COUNT [*throwing off his cloak and showing his magnificent habit*]: Ah, most adorable of women! The time has come to undeceive you. The happy man whom you see at your feet is no Lindor. I am Almaviva, and I love you to distraction. I have been searching for you in vain these six months past.

ROSINE [*falling into his arms*]: Ah!

THE COUNT [*alarmed*]: Figaro!

FIGARO: Nothing to worry about, My Lord. Happiness never did anyone any harm. See, she's coming round already. Gad! isn't she beautiful!

ROSINE: Ah, Lindor . . . Ah, Sir! How much I was to

blame! I was going to give myself to my guardian this very night.

THE COUNT: You were going to do what, Rosine?

ROSINE: Only think what my punishment would have been! I should have spent my whole life in hating you. Ah, Lindor! Isn't that the most dreadful fate imaginable – to hate when one knows that love is what one is made for?

FIGARO [*looking at the window*]: My Lord, escape is cut off! Someone has removed the ladder.

THE COUNT: Removed the ladder!

ROSINE [*in concern*]: Yes, I did it . . . it's the Doctor. This is the consequence of my credulity. He deceived me and I admitted everything. I told him of our plan. He knows that you are here and he will be bringing armed assistance. . . .

FIGARO [*looking out*]: My Lord, someone is opening the street door.

ROSINE [*running to his arms*]: Lindor!

THE COUNT [*with composure*]: Rosine. You love me! I fear no man living! You shall be my wife and I shall have the pleasure of punishing this odious old man to my heart's content.

ROSINE: No, no! Have mercy on him, dear Lindor. My heart is so full that vengeance can find no place there.

[*Enter* NOTARY *and* DON BAZILE.]

FIGARO: It's the notary, My Lord.

THE COUNT: And friend Bazile with him.

BAZILE: Ah! What's this I see?

FIGARO: What brings you here, friend?

BAZILE: What, gentlemen, how . . .

NOTARY: Are these the parties to the marriage?

THE COUNT: Yes, Sir. You were to have united Signora Rosine and myself tonight at Figaro's house, but we have decided to have the ceremony here for reasons you will be informed of later. Have you the contract ready?

NOTARY: Have I the honour to be addressing His Excellency Count Almaviva?

FIGARO: Precisely.

BAZILE [*aside*]: Is that why he gave me the master key?

NOTARY: I inquire because I have two marriage contracts prepared, My Lord. Let us not confuse them. Here is yours and here is one for Signor Bartholo with a lady – also called Rosine. Apparently the brides are sisters and bear the same name.

THE COUNT: Let us sign, nevertheless. Don Bazile will no doubt serve as our second witness.

[*They sign.*]

BAZILE: But ... Your Excellency ... I don't understand. ...

THE COUNT: My dear good Bazile, the slightest thing confuses you and everything fills you with astonishment.

BAZILE: My Lord – but if the Doctor ...

THE COUNT [*throwing him a purse*]: You are being childish. Sign at once.

BAZILE [*astonished*]: Oh! Ah!

FIGARO: What's the difficulty about signing?

BAZILE [*weighing the purse*]: No difficulty whatever now. It's like this with me – once I've given my word it takes a great deal to ... [*Signs.*]

[*Enter* BARTHOLO *with Alcalde and Alguazils and servants with lights.*

Seeing the COUNT *kissing Rosine's hand and* FIGARO *grotesquely embracing Don Bazile,* BARTHOLO *takes the notary by the throat.*]

BARTHOLO: Rosine with these scoundrels! Arrest the lot! I've got my hands on one of them!

NOTARY: I'm your notary.

BAZILE: He's your notary. Are you mad?

BARTHOLO: Ah, Don Bazile! How do you come to be here?

BAZILE: I might as well ask how do you come *not* to be here?

ALCALDE [*pointing to Figaro*]: One moment. I recognize this man. What are you doing here at this time of night?

FIGARO: Night? Your Worship can see it's nearer morning than night. For that matter I'm here in the company of His Excellency Count Almaviva.

BARTHOLO: Almaviva!

ALCALDE: They are not thieves then, after all?

BARTHOLO: We'll worry no more about that! [*To the Count*] Anywhere else, Your Excellency, I am your most humble servant, but you will agree that here in this house your superiority of rank carries no prerogative. Kindly have the goodness to retire.

THE COUNT: It is true that my rank carries no prerogative here. What gives me prerogative is this lady's preference, which she has just made clear by giving me – of her own free will – her hand.

BARTHOLO: What's this he says, Rosine?

ROSINE: What he says is the truth. Why are you so astonished? Did you not say yourself that I should be avenged on my deceiver this very night? I am.

BAZILE: Didn't I tell you it was the Count himself?

BARTHOLO: What's that to me! A farcical marriage! Where are the witnesses?

NOTARY: Everything is in due form. I had the assistance of these gentlemen.

BARTHOLO: What, Bazile – did you sign?

BAZILE: What do you expect? He's the very deuce of a fellow. He always has his pockets full of irresistible arguments.

BARTHOLO: I care nothing for his arguments. I rely on my authority as guardian.

THE COUNT: You forfeited it by abusing it.

BARTHOLO: The lady is a minor.

FIGARO: She's just come of age.

BARTHOLO: Who's talking to you – you arch-scoundrel?

THE COUNT: The lady is fair and of noble birth. I am a man of rank, young and rich. She is my wife. Does anyone presume to dispute a title which confers honour on both of us?

BARTHOLO: You'll never get her out of my hands.

THE COUNT: She is no longer in them. I place her under the jurisdiction of the law. The gentleman whom you yourself brought here will protect her from the violence you threaten her with. True magistrates are ever the defenders of the oppressed.

ALCALDE: True, and this futile resistance to a most honourable marriage is sufficient indication of his concern about his own ill-administration of his ward's possessions – for which he will be called to account.

THE COUNT: Ah! Let him give his consent and I ask nothing more.

FIGARO: Except acquittance of my hundred crowns. There's no point in losing our heads!

BARTHOLO: They are all against me. I've put my head into a hornet's nest.

BAZILE: Hornet's nest! No – remember, Doctor, though you lose the lady, you've still got her money. Oh, yes, you've still got her money!

BARTHOLO: Let me alone, Bazile. You can think of nothing but money. Much I care for *that*! I shall keep it all right, but do you think that's the motive that matters with me? [*He sighs.*]

FIGARO: There you see, My Lord! They are all alike when it comes to the point.

NOTARY: Gentlemen, I'm afraid I don't understand this at all. Are there not two ladies who bear the same name?

FIGARO: No, Sir. The two are one and the same.

BARTHOLO: And I took away the ladder thinking to make certain of marrying her. I lost for want of due care.

FIGARO: Want of good sense, you mean! We may be certain, Doctor, that when youth and love are at one anything that age may do to prevent them can only be described as a

FUTILE PRECAUTION

The Marriage of Figaro

OR

The Follies of a Day

CHARACTERS

COUNT ALMAVIVA, Governor of Andalusia

THE COUNTESS, his wife

FIGARO, his valet and major-domo

SUZANNE, maid to the Countess, betrothed to Figaro

MARCELINE, housekeeper

ANTONIO, gardener of the castle, uncle of Suzanne, and father of Fanchette

FANCHETTE, Antonio's daughter

CHÉRUBIN, a page

BARTHOLO, a doctor from Seville

BAZILE, music master to the Countess

DON GUZMAN BRID'OISON, a judge

DOUBLEMAIN, his clerk

GRIPE-SOLEIL, a shepherd lad

PEDRILLO, the Count's huntsman

An usher

A shepherdess

An alguazil

A magistrate

Servants, valets, peasants, and huntsmen

SCENE: *The castle of Aguas-Frescas, three leagues from Seville.*

ACT ONE

SCENE: *A bedroom partly stripped of furniture; a large high-backed chair in the middle.*

> [FIGARO *with a six-foot rule is measuring the floor.* SUZANNE *is trying on a wreath of orange blossom in front of the glass.*]

FIGARO: Nineteen feet by twenty-six.

SUZANNE: Look, Figaro. My wreath of orange blossom. Do you like it better so?

FIGARO [*taking her hands*]: Splendid, my darling! Oh! How precious in an adoring bridegroom's eyes is the charming virginal wreath that adorns the head of his beloved on her wedding morning.

SUZANNE: And what are you measuring there, my dear?

FIGARO: I'm just thinking about this fine bed which His Lordship is giving us. The question is – will it go here?

SUZANNE: In this room?

FIGARO: This is the one he's letting us have.

SUZANNE: Well *I* don't want it.

FIGARO: Why?

SUZANNE: I just don't.

FIGARO: But why not?

SUZANNE: I don't like it.

FIGARO: You might give a reason?

SUZANNE: Suppose I don't want to?

FIGARO: Ay! Once they are sure of us ...

SUZANNE: Giving a reason for being right amounts to admitting I could be wrong. Are you my humble servitor or aren't you?

FIGARO: Why take a prejudice against the room? It's the most convenient one in the castle, and it's in between the two suites of rooms. Suppose My Lady wants something in the night – she rings from her side – Hey presto! A couple of steps and you are in her room. On the other hand, should His Lordship want anything he need only give a tinkle and lo and behold! A hop and a skip and I'm there.

SUZANNE: Very nice too! But suppose he has given a tinkle in the morning and sent you off on some lengthy task – Hey presto! A couple of steps and he's at my door. Then lo and behold! A hop and a skip . . .

FIGARO: Whatever *are* you talking about?

SUZANNE: Why don't you listen?

FIGARO: But good Lord! What is it all about?

SUZANNE: This is what it's about, my dear boy – My Lord the Count, tired of cultivating rustic beauties, has a mind to return to the castle but not to his wife: it's yours he has cast his eye on, understand, and he thinks that this room might well prove quite convenient; so the ever-loyal Bazile, faithful agent of his master's pleasures and my esteemed singing teacher, daily suggests to me as he gives me my lesson.

FIGARO: Ah! Friend Bazile! If a good stout cudgel properly applied to anyone's back and shoulders could . . .

SUZANNE: You didn't think, silly boy, that this dowry I am to receive was a tribute to your own outstanding merits?

FIGARO: I have done sufficient to hope so.

SUZANNE: How stupid clever men can be!

FIGARO: So they say.

SUZANNE: Yes, but some people are unwilling to believe it.

FIGARO: That's where you are wrong.

SUZANNE: Let me tell you – he means to use it some time when he gets me alone for a few minutes to exact an ancient *Droit de Seigneur* . . . you know what that means.

FIGARO: So much so that if His Lordship hadn't abolished

the infamous privilege when he got married himself I would never have married you within his domains.

SUZANNE: Very well! He may have abolished it, but now he wishes he hadn't and it's with your bride-to-be that he means to revive it today.

FIGARO [*rubbing his forehead*]: I'm quite dizzy with the shock – and my forehead is sprouting . . . already . . .

SUZANNE: Don't rub it then.

FIGARO: There's no danger, is there?

SUZANNE: If there were to be the slightest little swelling . . . superstitious people . . .

FIGARO: You are laughing at me, you witch! Ah! If only there were some means of catching out this arch-deceiver, of leading him into a trap and pocketing his money.

SUZANNE: Intrigue and money – you are in your element now.

FIGARO: It isn't any sense of shame that restrains me.

SUZANNE: What is it, then, fear?

FIGARO: There's nothing in taking risks, but to take risks and at the same time turn them to your advantage – that's something! To enter some fellow's house at night, do him down with his wife, and to get a good hiding for your pains – nothing easier: a thousand blundering boobies have done it but . . .

[*Bell within.*]

SUZANNE: That means Her Ladyship is awake. She asked me to be the first person to speak to her on my wedding morning.

FIGARO: Has that some significance as well?

SUZANNE: There's an old saying that it brings luck to neglected wives. Good-bye, dear Fi-Fi-Figaro! Think about our little problem.

FIGARO: What about a kiss to encourage me?

SUZANNE: From my lover of today? I should think not! What will my husband say about it tomorrow?

[FIGARO *kisses her.*]

SUZANNE: There! There!

FIGARO: You just have no idea how I love you.

SUZANNE [*disengaging herself*]: When are you going to give up telling me so from morning to night, stupid?

FIGARO: When I can prove it from night until morning.

[*A second ring.*]

SUZANNE [*finger-tips to her lips*]: There's your kiss back, Sir. I want nothing more of you now.

FIGARO [*running after her*]: But you didn't say that when I gave it you.

[*Exit* SUZANNE.]

FIGARO: Dear charming girl! For ever laughing, blooming, full of gaiety and wit, loving and wholly delightful! And yet prudent. [*Walks up and down rubbing his forehead.*] And so, Your Lordship, you would do me down, would you! I wondered why, having put me in charge of the household, he wanted to take me with him on his embassy and make me his courier. I have got the idea, Your Highness! It's a triple promotion! You – Minister Plenipotentiary, me – the breakneck postilion, Suzie – lady of the back stairs and pocket ambassadress! And then, off you go, courier! While I'm galloping in one direction you'll be progressing nicely in another – with my little wife! I shall be fighting my way through rain and mud for the greater glory of your family while you are condescending to cooperate in the increase of mine. A pretty sort of reciprocity! But it's going too far, My Lord! To be doing both your master's job and your valet's at the same time, representing the King – and my-self – at a foreign court is overdoing it. It's too much by half! As for you, Bazile, you dirty old dog, I'll teach you to run with the hounds, I'll – no, we shall have to dissimulate if we are to use one against the other. Look to the day's work, Master Figaro! First bring forward the hour of your wedding to make sure of the ceremony taking place, head off Marceline who's so deucedly fond of you, pocket the money and the presents, thwart His Lordship's little game, give Master Bazile a good thrashing, and . . .

[*Enter* MARCELINE *and* BARTHOLO.]

Ha! Ha! Here comes the portly doctor; now the party will be complete! Hello! Good day to you, my dear doctor. Is it my marriage with Suzanne that brings you to the castle?

BARTHOLO [*disdainful*]: Not at all, my good sir, not at all.

FIGARO: That would be very generous on your part.

BARTHOLO: It would indeed – too absurd for anything.

FIGARO: I having had the misfortune to thwart your own marriage.

BARTHOLO: Have you anything else to say?

FIGARO: Are they taking care of your mule?

BARTHOLO [*enraged*]: Incorrigible babbler! Leave us!

FIGARO: You are not annoyed, Doctor, are you? Men in your position are very hard – no pity for poor animals, no more than if they were men! Good day to you, Marceline! Are you still anxious to put me in court?

'Because one loves not – must one loathe oneself?'

I leave it to the doctor.

BARTHOLO: What's that?

FIGARO: She'll tell you about it – and a lot more.

[*Exit* FIGARO.]

BARTHOLO [*watching him go*]: Just the same scoundrel as ever! If he escapes the gallows I predict that he'll end up as the most insolent, outrageous . . .

MARCELINE [*turns him about*]: There you are! The everlasting Doctor! Always so grave and formal that one might die waiting for your help just as a certain person once got married in spite of all your precautions.

BARTHOLO: Nasty-minded and spiteful as ever! Anyhow, why is my presence required at the castle? Has My Lord the Count had some mishap?

MARCELINE: No, Doctor.

BARTHOLO: Rosine, his deceitful Countess, is perhaps unwell, Heaven be praised!

MARCELINE: She's listless, languishing, pining away.

BARTHOLO: What's wrong with her?

MARCELINE: Her husband neglects her.

BARTHOLO [*with satisfaction*]: Ah! Noble husband! He avenges me.

MARCELINE: One doesn't know just how to describe the Count. He's both dissolute and jealous.

BARTHOLO: Dissolute from boredom. Jealous from vanity. That goes without saying.

MARCELINE: Today, for example, he's giving our Suzanne in marriage to his man Figaro. The union is a method of showing his favour.

BARTHOLO: A union which His Excellency has made necessary?

MARCELINE: Not entirely, but one His Excellency would like a share in celebrating with the bride.

BARTHOLO: Of Master Figaro? No doubt an arrangement could be made.

MARCELINE: Bazile says not.

BARTHOLO: Is that scoundrel here too? It's a den of thieves. What's he doing here?

MARCELINE: All the mischief he can. The worst thing from my point of view is the tiresome fancy he's so long had for me.

BARTHOLO: You could easily get rid of his attentions.

MARCELINE: How?

BARTHOLO: By marrying him.

MARCELINE: Cruel mocker! Why didn't you get rid of mine

in the same way? Wasn't that what you ought to have done? Have you no memory for your obligations? What became of our little Emmanuel, fruit of a forgotten passion that should have led us to the altar?

BARTHOLO [*taking off his hat*]: Did you have me come from Seville to listen to this sort of nonsense? If you are so full of enthusiasm for marriage . . .

MARCELINE: All right. We'll say no more about it. But since nothing could induce you to do the right thing and marry me, at least help me to marry someone else.

BARTHOLO: By all means! Let us discuss it. But what mortal, abandoned of gods and women, could . . . it be?

MARCELINE: Why! Who else could it be but the gay, handsome Figaro?

BARTHOLO: That worthless scoundrel!

MARCELINE: Never angry, always good-humoured, living for the pleasure of the moment, worrying as little about the future as the past, carefree and . . . generous . . . generous as . . .

BARTHOLO: As a thief!

MARCELINE: As a lord! He's utterly charming! Yet he's a cruel monster.

BARTHOLO: And his Suzanne?

MARCELINE: She shall never have him, cunning little thing though she is, if you'll help me, Doctor, to enforce an obligation he has to me.

BARTHOLO: What! On his wedding day?

MARCELINE: It's never too late to break 'em off. If it weren't for giving away feminine secrets . . .

BARTHOLO: Do women have any secrets from their doctors?

MARCELINE: Ah! You know that I have none from you! Our sex is ardent but timid. However much we are attracted to pleasure, the most venturesome of women hears a voice within her say, 'Be fair if you can, wise if you will, but be circumspect you must.' So, since one must at least be circumspect as every woman realizes – let us first frighten Suzanne about any possible disclosure of the offers which are being made to her.

BARTHOLO: Where does that lead us to?

MARCELINE: Shame will drive her to persist in saying 'no' to the Count, who in revenge will throw his weight against the marriage: and so mine will be assured.

BARTHOLO: By Jove, she's right! It would be a good stroke to marry off my old governess to the rascal who helped to rob me of my young mistress.

MARCELINE: And hoped to add to his own pleasure by disappointing me.

BARTHOLO: And once robbed me of a hundred crowns, as I still haven't forgotten.

MARCELINE: Ah, what a satisfaction it will be!

BARTHOLO: To punish a scoundrel.

MARCELINE: To marry him, Doctor! To marry him!

   [*Enter* SUZANNE, *carrying a hat with a wide ribbon and a dress on her arm.*]

SUZANNE: 'To marry him! To marry him!' Who? My Figaro?

MARCELINE [*bitterly*]: Why not? You are for marrying him, aren't you?

BARTHOLO [*laughing*]: Now for a fine slanging-match between two angry women! We were saying, my dear Suzie, how fortunate he'll be in possessing a girl such as you.

MARCELINE: Not to mention my Lord the Count!

SUZANNE [*curtseying*]: Your servant, Madam! There's always something nasty about your remarks.

MARCELINE [*curtseying*]: And I, yours! What is there nasty in that, may I ask? Isn't it right and proper that so liberal a nobleman should have a share in the happiness he procures for his servants?

SUZANNE: Procures?

MARCELINE: That was the word I used.

SUZANNE: Fortunately your jealousy is as notorious as your claims on Figaro are slight.

MARCELINE: I might have strengthened them had I cared to cement them by the same methods as yours.

SUZANNE: Oh! The methods are well known to ladies of your learning and experience.

MARCELINE: And you have no experience? Innocent as sin, eh?

BARTHOLO [*drawing Marceline away*]: Good-bye, sweetheart of Master Figaro.

MARCELINE [*curtseying*]: And object of My Lord's secret understanding.

SUZANNE [*curtseying*]: Who holds you in the highest esteem.

MARCELINE [*curtseying*]: Will she not do me the honour of adding a measure of affection?

SUZANNE [*curtseying*]: You may be sure that I leave you nothing to desire in that respect, Madam.

MARCELINE [*curtseying*]: Such a pretty young lady!

SUZANNE [*curtseying*]: Sufficiently so to spoil your satisfaction –

MARCELINE [*curtseying*]: And above all so careful of her reputation –

SUZANNE [*curtseying*]: Reputation one leaves to duennas.

MARCELINE [*outraged*]: Duennas! To duennas!

BARTHOLO [*checking her*]: Marceline!

MARCELINE: Let us go, Doctor. Or I shan't be able to control myself. Good day to you, Madam. [*Curtseys.*]

    [*Exeunt* MARCELINE *and* BARTHOLO.]

SUZANNE: Be off! Be off, you pedantic old hag! Little I care for you or your insults. The old witch! Because she has had some education and made her Ladyship miserable when she was young she wants to domineer over the whole castle.

[*Throws dress on chair.*] I don't remember what I came in for.

CHÉRUBIN [*running in*]: Ah, Suzie, I've been waiting this last hour for a chance to catch you alone. Alas, you are getting married and I'm going away!

SUZANNE: What has my marriage to do with the departure of His Lordship's favourite page?

CHÉRUBIN [*pitifully*]: Suzanne, he's sending me away.

SUZANNE [*imitating him*]: Chérubin, have you done something silly again?

CHÉRUBIN: He caught me with your cousin Fanchette yesterday evening. I was putting her through her part for tonight. He was furious when he saw me. 'Get out,' he said, 'you little –' I daren't repeat the rude word he used to a lady. 'Get out – you ... You shan't sleep another night in the castle!' It's all up, Suzanne, unless Her Ladyship, my dear godmother, can get him to relent. I shall never, never see you any more.

SUZANNE: See me? So it's my turn now, is it? It's no longer the Mistress you are secretly sighing for?

CHÉRUBIN: Ah, Suzie! She's noble and beautiful, but how unapproachable!

SUZANNE: You mean that I'm not, and with me you dare hope. . . .

CHÉRUBIN: You know only too well, you naughty thing, that I daren't hope for anything at all! But how lucky you are! To see her all the time, to talk to her, to dress her in the morning and undress her at night – one pin after another – Ah, Suzie! I'd give ... What's that you have there?

SUZANNE [*teasing him*]: Alas! the fortunate night-cap and the equally fortunate ribbon that does up your fair godmother's hair for the night.

CHÉRUBIN: Her ribbon! Give it me, sweetheart!

SUZANNE: Oh, no, you don't! Sweetheart forsooth! How

familiar he's getting! If only he weren't just a snotty little good-for-nothing! Ah! [*As* CHÉRUBIN *snatches it*] The ribbon!

CHÉRUBIN [*dodging round the large chair*]: You can say that it got torn, dirty, lost, anything you like.

SUZANNE [*chasing him*]: Oh, what a worthless scamp you'll be when you are a year or two older! Give me the ribbon! [*Tries to get it.*]

CHÉRUBIN [*taking a sheet of music from his pocket*]: Leave go! Ah! Let me go, Suzie! I'll give you my ballad, and when the memory of your beautiful mistress saddens my days thoughts of you will be my one consolation.

SUZANNE: Your one consolation, you young scamp! Do you think you are talking to that Fanchette of yours? You are caught with her yet you'll sigh for your Mistress. Now on top of all that you are trying it on with me.

CHÉRUBIN [*exalted*]: Upon my word it's quite true! I don't know what's coming over me. For some time I have had such a strange feeling within me. My pulse quickens at the very sight of a woman. The word love makes my heart go pit-a-pat. In fact, I feel such a need to say 'I love you' to someone that I catch myself saying it to myself walking in the park, to your Mistress, to you, to the trees, to the clouds, to the wind which wafts them away with my fleeting words. Yesterday I met Marceline. . . .

SUZANNE [*laughing*]: Ha ha ha!

CHÉRUBIN: Why not? She's a woman. Woman – girl – maiden! How thrilling the words are!

SUZANNE: He's going dippy!

CHÉRUBIN: Fanchette is kind. She does listen to me! You aren't kind at all.

SUZANNE: A pity, isn't it? Now listen, young man! [*She tries to snatch the ribbon.*]

CHÉRUBIN [*dodges away*]: Ah, would you! Only over my dead

117

body! If that's not enough shall we say . . . plus a thousand kisses? [*He chases her now.*]

SUZANNE [*dodges him*]: Plus a thousand slaps if you come near me. I shall complain to the Mistress. So far from interceding for you I'll say to his Lordship, 'You did well, my Lord! Send him away – the little thief! Send him home to his family, the nasty little thing! He has the audacity to be in love with his Mistress and yet wants to be kissing me too.'

[CHÉRUBIN, *seeing the* COUNT *enter, throws himself behind the chair in terror.*]

CHÉRUBIN: I'm done for!

SUZANNE [*not seeing the Count*]: What's frightening him? [*Seeing the Count*] Oh! [*Goes to the chair to hide Chérubin.*]

THE COUNT: You are excited, Suzie! Talking to yourself and your little heart going pit-a-pat . . . very understandable of course on such a day. . . .

SUZANNE [*in concern*]: What do you want of me, My Lord? Suppose anyone found you here with me. . . .

THE COUNT: I should be very sorry indeed if they did. But you know what an interest I take in you. Bazile must have let you know of my love for you. I have only a moment to explain what I have in mind. Listen. [*Sits on chair.*]

SUZANNE: I won't listen!

THE COUNT [*takes her hand*]: You know that the King has appointed me his ambassador in London. I'm taking Figaro with me. I'm giving him an excellent job, and as a wife's duty is to follow her husband . . .

SUZANNE: Ah! If only I dare speak!

THE COUNT [*drawing her to him*]: Speak. Speak, my dear! Take advantage here and now of your influence over me, an influence that will endure. . . .

SUZANNE [*alarmed*]: I wish for none, Sir. I wish for none! Leave me, I beseech you!

THE COUNT: But tell me first. . . .

SUZANNE [*angrily*]: I don't remember what I was saying. . . .

THE COUNT: We were talking of wifely duty. . . .

SUZANNE: Very well. Since your Lordship rescued your own wife from the Doctor and married her for love – since you abolished at her instance a certain horrible privilege . . .

THE COUNT [*gaily*]: To the great disappointment of the girls! Ah, Suzie! A charming custom! If only you would come and talk about it with me this evening in the garden I would make the favour so worth while that . . .

BAZILE [*off-stage*]: He's not at home, Sir.

THE COUNT [*rising*]: Whose voice was that?

SUZANNE: Ah, unhappy me!

THE COUNT: Go, in case anyone comes in.

SUZANNE [*worried*]: And leave you here?

BAZILE: His Lordship was with My Lady. He's out – I'll go and inquire.

THE COUNT: Nowhere to hide. Ah, behind the armchair! That's not much good. Send him away quickly.

[SUZANNE *bars his way. He pushes her gently. She recoils but still puts herself between him and the page. As the* COUNT *crouches down* CHÉRUBIN *turns and throws himself into the chair in a kneeling position and hides his head in terror.* SUZANNE *takes the dress she is carrying, covers him up, and stands in front of the chair.*

Enter BAZILE.]

BAZILE: Haven't you seen His Lordship, Miss?

SUZANNE [*sharply*]: Why should I have seen him? Get out.

BAZILE [*still coming forward*]: If only you were more reasonable you would see that there's nothing surprising in my question. It's Figaro who's looking for him.

SUZANNE: Then he's looking for the man who next after you wishes him most harm.

THE COUNT [*aside*]: We shall see now what sort of servant I have.

BAZILE: So – to wish a woman well is to wish her husband harm?

SUZANNE: Not according to your horrible ideas – agent of corruption that you are!

BAZILE: What is being asked of you that you aren't going to lavish on another? Thanks to one little ceremony, what is forbidden you today will be required of you tomorrow.

SUZANNE: Shame!

BAZILE: Considering what a farce it is to take marriage so seriously, I had in mind . . .

SUZANNE: Horrible things, no doubt! Anyhow who gives you permission to come in here?

BAZILE: There, there, Spitfire! May Heaven teach you patience! You shall have it your own way; but don't think that I regard Master Figaro as any obstacle in My Lord's way. As for that little page . . .

SUZANNE [*timidly*]: What, Master Chérubin?

BAZILE [*imitating her*]: *Cherubino di amore*, that dear little cherub who's always hanging round you and only this morning was prowling about here waiting to get in when I left you – that's true, isn't it?

SUZANNE: What a tale! Go away, horrid man!

BAZILE: Because I don't go about with my eyes shut I'm a horrid man. Wasn't this ballad he makes such a fuss about intended for you?

SUZANNE [*annoyed*]: Oh, of course! For me, indeed!

BAZILE: Always assuming he didn't write it for Her Ladyship. They say he can't keep his eyes off her when he's serving at table. My goodness! Don't let him play any tricks in that quarter! His Lordship has no mercy on that sort of thing.

SUZANNE [*outraged*]: Are you knave enough to go spreading

gossip to ruin an unfortunate lad who's already in disgrace with his master!

BAZILE: Did I invent it? I'm only repeating what everybody's saying.

THE COUNT [*springing to his feet*]: And what *is* everybody saying?

SUZANNE: Oh heavens!

BAZILE: Ha! Ha!

THE COUNT: Off you go, Bazile. Have him turned out at once.

BAZILE: Ah! How I wish I hadn't come in!

SUZANNE [*thoroughly alarmed*]: Oh, my goodness!

THE COUNT [*to Bazile*]: She's fainting. Sit her down in the chair.

SUZANNE [*pushing him away vigorously*]: I don't want to sit down. Fancy his coming in like that! It's disgusting!

THE COUNT: There are two of us here, my dear. There's not the slightest danger now.

BAZILE: I'm sorry I made a joke about the page, since you could hear me: I only did it to find out what she really thought. At bottom . . .

THE COUNT: Give him fifty crowns and a horse, and send him home to his family.

BAZILE: But My Lord – all because of a joke?

THE COUNT: The little reprobate! I've already surprised him once today with the gardener's daughter.

BAZILE: With Fanchette?

THE COUNT: In her bedroom, at that!

SUZANNE [*scandalized*]· Where My Lord no doubt had business as well!

THE COUNT [*gaily*]: I like that!

BAZILE: It's a good augury!

THE COUNT [*gaily*]: No. I went there to look for your uncle Antonio, my drunkard of a gardener, to give him his instructions. I knock. It's some time before the door is opened: your cousin looks a bit embarrassed and I become suspicious. Still carrying on the conversation I take a look round. There's a sort of curtain behind the door – a wardrobe of some sort. Slowly and stealthily I lift the curtain [*showing how by lifting the dress from the chair*] and what do I see? [*Perceives the page.*] Ah!

BAZILE: Ha! Ha!

THE COUNT: Just like the last time!

BAZILE: Better!

THE COUNT [*to Suzanne*]: Very nice, too! Not even married yet and already up to all the tricks! You wanted to be alone so that you could receive my page, eh? As for you, Sir, your behaviour's all of a piece. You have so little respect for your mistress as to address your attentions to her maid, to the wife of your friend. But I won't allow Figaro, a man I love and esteem, to be a victim of such deception. Was he with you, Bazile?

SUZANNE [*furious*]: There was no deception and no victim. He was there all the time you were talking to me.

THE COUNT [*equally furious in his turn*]: How can you tell such an untruth? His worst enemy wouldn't wish him such a misfortune.

SUZANNE: He was asking me to get Her Ladyship to intervene on his behalf. He was so frightened by your arrival that he hid behind the chair.

THE COUNT: What a diabolical fib! I sat in it when I came in.

CHÉRUBIN: Alas, My Lord! I was shivering behind it.

THE COUNT: Another fabrication! I have just been behind it myself.

CHÉRUBIN: Pardon me, but it was then that I hid myself in it.

THE COUNT [*more enraged than ever*]: Then the little snake overheard all we said!

CHÉRUBIN: On the contrary, My Lord, I did my best not to hear anything.

THE COUNT: Oh, the perfidy! [*To Suzanne*] You shan't marry Figaro, now.

BAZILE: Hush! There's somebody coming.

THE COUNT [*picking Chérubin up and setting him on his feet*]: He shall stand there for all the world to see.

[*Enter the* COUNTESS, FIGARO, FANCHETTE, *and peasants all in white.*]

FIGARO [*carrying a woman's headress trimmed with white feathers and ribbons – addressing the Countess*]: No one but Your Ladyship can obtain this favour for us.

THE COUNTESS: You see what they are, My Lord – they credit me with an influence which I do not enjoy. But since what they ask is not unreasonable . . .

THE COUNT [*embarrassed*]: It would have to be very much so before . . .

FIGARO [*aside to Suzanne*]: Back me up!

SUZANNE [*aside to Figaro*]: No use!

FIGARO [*as before*]: Try, all the same.

THE COUNT [*to Figaro*]: Well? What do you want?

FIGARO: My Lord! Your vassals, gratified by the abolition of a certain objectionable privilege which you, in your affection for My Lady . . .

THE COUNT: Very well! The privilege is abolished. What do you want to say?

FIGARO [*shyly*]: That it is high time that the virtues of so good a Master were publicly acclaimed. Since I derive such signal benefit from it today, I would like my marriage to be the first celebration of it.

THE COUNT [*more embarrassed still*]: You are mistaken, my friend. The abolition of a shameful custom is no more than an acknowledgement of what is due to common decency. A Spaniard may aspire to achieve the conquest of beauty by his own assiduities, but to exact the first, the most precious enjoyment of it as a servile requirement – that's the tyranny of a vandal, not the privilege of a noble Castilian.

FIGARO [*taking Suzanne by the hand*]: Permit, then, that this young lady, whose honour your wisdom has preserved, may publicly receive at your hands, as a symbol of the purity of your intentions, this virginal toque adorned with white feathers and ribbons: accept this ceremony for all future marriages, and may these verses which we sing in chorus for ever preserve the memory . . .

THE COUNT [*embarrassed*]: If I didn't know that lover, poet, and musician are the three titles of indulgence for every sort of folly and . . .

FIGARO: Join with me, friends!

ALL: His Lordship! His Lordship!

SUZANNE [*to the Count*]: Why seek to avoid a tribute you have so well deserved?

THE COUNT [*aside*]: Perfidious creature!

FIGARO: Look at her, My Lord! No fairer bride will ever exemplify the magnitude of your sacrifice.

SUZANNE: Stop talking about me and concentrate on praising his virtue.

THE COUNT [*aside*]: What a game!

THE COUNTESS: My Lord, I join my plea to theirs. I shall always cherish the memory of a ceremony which has its origins in the love you once bore me.

THE COUNT: And still do, Madam, and to that consideration I yield.

ALL: *Vivat!*

THE COUNT [*aside*]: I'm caught! [*Aloud*] I would only suggest that the ceremony may be postponed until later in order that it may be more effectively known. [*Aside to Bazile*] Quick – get them to find Marceline.

FIGARO [*to Chérubin*]: Hey, you scamp! Why aren't you applauding?

SUZANNE: He's in despair. His Lordship has banished him.

THE COUNTESS: Ah, Sir! I ask your clemency on his behalf.

THE COUNT: He doesn't deserve it.

THE COUNTESS: Alas! He's so young.

THE COUNT: Not so young as you think.

CHÉRUBIN [*trembling*]: The right to pardon generously was not the one you renounced when you married Her Ladyship.

SUZANNE: If the right to pardon were the one His Lordship had renounced it would surely be the first one he would wish to resume.

THE COUNT [*embarrassed*]: Of course!

THE COUNTESS: Then what need to resume it?

CHÉRUBIN [*to the Count*]: It's true, My Lord, that I acted unwisely, but I never talked indiscreetly.

THE COUNT: All right – that's enough.

FIGARO: What does he mean?

THE COUNT: Enough, enough! Everybody wants him forgiven. I agree and I'll go further. I'll give him a company in my own regiment.

ALL: *Vivat!*

THE COUNT: On condition that he leaves for Catalonia to join it immediately.

FIGARO: Ah, My Lord! Tomorrow!

THE COUNT: Immediately – that is my decision.

CHÉRUBIN: I obey.

THE COUNT: Say farewell to your godmother and ask her to pray for your protection.

[CHÉRUBIN *goes on one knee before the Countess, but cannot find words to speak.*]

THE COUNTESS [*moved*]: Go, young man, since we may not keep you even for today. Destiny calls: go and fill it worthily. Do credit to your benefactor. Remember this house where your youth has found such indulgence. Be obedient, honourable, and brave; we shall rejoice in your successes.

[CHÉRUBIN *rises and returns to his place.*]

THE COUNT: Your Ladyship is greatly moved.

THE COUNTESS: I don't deny it. Who knows what may be the fate of a boy thrown into a career of such danger. He is my kinsman and, what is more, my godchild.

THE COUNT [*aside*]: I see that Bazile was right. [*To Chérubin*] Young man, salute Suzanne for the last time.

FIGARO: But why the last time, Your Highness? He'll come here during his winter leave. . . . Kiss me too, Captain! [*He embraces him.*] Good-bye, my dear Chérubin. You are going to a very different life. By Jove, yes! No more running round all day with the girls, no more cream buns and custard tarts; no more 'tig' and blind-man's-buff. Soldiers of the Queen, by Gad! Just think of 'em, weather-beaten and ragged arsed, weighed down with their muskets, right turn, left wheel, forward march! On to the field of glory and no flinching on the way – unless a round of shot . . .

SUZANNE: Oh! For goodness' sake!

THE COUNTESS: What a prospect!

THE COUNT: Where is Marceline? It's very strange that she's not with you people.

FANCHETTE: She's gone into the town by the little path by the farm.

THE COUNT: When will she be back?

BAZILE: In God's good time.

FIGARO: If only he'd keep her away for good!

FANCHETTE: The Doctor was with her.

THE COUNT [*sharply*]: The Doctor is here, is he?

FANCHETTE: She button-holed him as soon as he arrived.

THE COUNT [*aside*]: He couldn't have come at a better time.

FANCHETTE: She seemed to be very annoyed about something. She was talking loudly as they went along and then she stopped and did like this – with open arms, and the doctor did like this – trying to calm her down: she seemed to be terribly angry and kept mentioning cousin Figaro.

THE COUNT [*chin on hand*]: Cousin – future husband –

FANCHETTE [*pointing to Chérubin*]: My Lord! Have you forgiven us for yesterday?

THE COUNT [*interrupting*]: That's all right, that's all right, my dear!

FIGARO: She's brooding on her confounded affection for me! She wanted to upset our wedding. . . .

THE COUNT [*aside*]: She'll upset it yet, I promise you. . . . [*Aloud*] Let us go in, Madam. Bazile, I shall want you.

SUZANNE [*to Figaro*]: Are you coming back to see me?

FIGARO [*whispers*]: Have you got him on the hook?

SUZANNE: Silly boy!

> [*All go out. As they are going* FIGARO *stops Chérubin and Bazile and brings them back.*]

FIGARO: Now, you two. One stage of the ceremony over, my celebrations follow this evening. Let's run over our plans; don't let us be like some actors who never perform so badly as the day when the critics are all there in force. There's no chance of doing this better another time. Let us know our parts properly today.

BAZILE [*significantly*]: Mine's more difficult than you would think.

FIGARO [*making a gesture of hitting him without his seeing it*]: Ah! But you little know what reward it will bring you.

CHÉRUBIN: But, my dear Figaro, you forget that I'm leaving.

FIGARO: And you would rather stay?

CHÉRUBIN: Ah! If only I could!

FIGARO: We must dissemble. Not a word of complaint about having to go. Put your travelling coat over your arm, do all your packing: let your horse be seen at the gate, gallop as far as the farm, return on foot the back way. His Lordship will think you are gone: just take care to keep out of his sight and leave it to me to pacify him after the celebrations.

CHÉRUBIN: But Fanchette doesn't know her part.

BAZILE: Then what the deuce have you been teaching her the last week? You've been with her all the time!

FIGARO: You've nothing to do today: give her an additional lesson.

BAZILE: Be careful, young man! Be careful! Her father isn't pleased: the girl's had her ears boxed: it's not study she's been doing with you. Oh, Chérubin! You'll get yourself into trouble one of these days. The pitcher can go to the well, you know. . . .

FIGARO: Listen to the old fool and his proverbs. All right, you old pedant, what does the wisdom of the ages say? The pitcher can go to the well – and what happens?

BAZILE: It gets filled.

FIGARO [going]: Not too bad! Not too bad!

ACT TWO

SCENE: *A bedroom furnished with great splendour; a bed in a recess; a dais downstage of it; a door upstage right; door to a small closet downstage left; door upstage to the maid's quarters; window at the other side.*

[SUZANNE *and the* COUNTESS *enter from the right.*]

THE COUNTESS [*throwing herself into an easy-chair*]: Close the door, Suzanne, and tell me exactly what happened.

SUZANNE: I have withheld nothing from you, Madam.

THE COUNTESS: You really mean to say, Suzie, that he was endeavouring to seduce you?

SUZANNE: Not at all! His Lordship doesn't put himself to so much trouble as that with a servant: he merely wanted a financial arrangement.

THE COUNTESS: And the page was there all the time?

SUZANNE: Behind the armchair in fact. He had come to ask me to persuade you to intercede for him.

THE COUNTESS: Why didn't he come to me? Should I have refused him, Suzie?

SUZANNE: That's what I told him: but he was so distressed at leaving and particularly at parting from Your Ladyship ... 'Ah! Suzie! How noble and beautiful she is! But how unapproachable!'

THE COUNTESS: Do I really seem like that, Suzie? I, who have always been his protector.

SUZANNE: He no sooner saw your ribbon which I had in my hand than he fairly leapt at it.

THE COUNTESS [*smiling*]: My ribbon! What childishness!

SUZANNE: I tried to get it back from him. He fought like a

129

lion, Your Ladyship. His eyes flashed. 'Over my dead body!' he said in his shrill high-pitched voice.

THE COUNTESS [*lost in thought*]: And then, Suzie?

SUZANNE: And then, Madam? What can you do with such a young demon? On the one hand, respect for his godmother, on the other – 'If only I could –' And because he daren't even venture to kiss the hem of Your Ladyship's gown he wanted to embrace me, if you please!

THE COUNTESS [*still dreaming*]: A truce to these foolish things. So, my dear Suzanne, my husband ended by telling you –

SUZANNE: That if I wouldn't listen to him he would support Marceline. . . .

THE COUNTESS [*rising and walking up and down fanning herself*]: He no longer loves me.

SUZANNE: Then why is he so jealous?

THE COUNTESS: Like all husbands, my dear – from pride – nothing more. Ah, I have loved him too dearly! I have wearied him with my solicitude and tired him with my love. That's the only offence I have been guilty of: but I don't intend to let you suffer for having rebuffed him: you shall marry your Figaro. He's the one person who can help us. Is he coming back?

SUZANNE: When he's seen the hunt move off.

THE COUNTESS [*fanning herself*]: Open the window a little. It's hot in here.

SUZANNE: Your Ladyship takes so much out of herself. [*Opens window upstage.*]

THE COUNTESS [*dreaming*]: Men are all the same. . . . Were it not for his persistence in avoiding me . . .

SUZANNE: Ah, there goes His Lordship riding across the park with Pedrillo and two, three – four greyhounds.

THE COUNTESS: Then we have time still. [*Sits down.*] Was that someone knocking, Suzie?

SUZANNE [*running to open the door, saying*]: Ah! It's my Figaro! My Figaro! Do come in, my dear! Her Ladyship is anxious to see you.

FIGARO: And how about you, my dear Suzanne? There's no need for Her Ladyship to worry. What, in fact, does it amount to? A mere nothing! His Lordship finds a young woman attractive: he would like to make her his mistress. It's all very natural.

SUZANNE: Natural?

FIGARO: So he appoints me his courier and Suzie Counsellor to the Embassy. . . . Not a bad idea at all, is it?

SUZANNE: Oh, do give up!

FIGARO: And now because Suzanne, my fiancée, doesn't accept the honour he confers on her, he proposes to take up the cause of Marceline. What could be simpler? Somebody thwarts one's plans so one gets one's own back by upsetting theirs. Everybody does it – and it's what we are going to do too. That's all there is to it.

THE COUNTESS: Figaro! How can you treat so lightly a scheme which threatens the happiness of every one of us?

FIGARO: Who says I do so, Your Ladyship?

SUZANNE: Instead of taking our troubles to heart . . .

FIGARO: Isn't it sufficient that I take them in hand? No, if we are to go about things as methodically as he does, let us discourage his ardour for what is ours by giving him cause for concern for what is his.

THE COUNTESS: All very well. But how?

FIGARO: It's already done, Your Ladyship – a false report about you . . . a trifling scandal . . .

THE COUNTESS: About me? Are you out of your mind?

FIGARO: *He* must be!

THE COUNTESS: A man so jealous as . . .

FIGARO: So much the better: if you are to cope with such people what you need to do is to get them annoyed. How well women understand that! Once you get a man thoroughly enraged, a little manoeuvring and you can do what you like with him – lead him into the Guadalquivir if you want to. I have arranged for Bazile to receive a letter from an unseen hand warning His Lordship that a young man intends to meet you tonight at the ball.

THE COUNTESS: You'll play tricks with truth which involve a virtuous woman ...

FIGARO: There are few, Madam, with whom I would have dared take the risk – lest it might prove to be true.

THE COUNTESS: I suppose I'm to be thankful for that!

FIGARO: But don't you think it's considerate of me to have arranged his little day for him so that he'll spend his time rushing round and cursing his own wife when he meant to be ingratiating himself with mine? He's already quite beside himself. He's galloping here, searching there, and worried to death! Look! There he goes – charging across country after a poor helpess hare. The time for the wedding will soon be here and he'll have done nothing to prevent it and won't dare to in Your Ladyship's presence.

SUZANNE: No, but that old blue stocking, Marceline, will.

FIGARO: Pah! A lot that worries me! You must send word to His Lordship that you'll meet him at dusk in the garden.

SUZANNE: You are still relying on that idea?

FIGARO: Oh, confound it, listen to me! Folk who won't try never get anywhere. That's my opinion.

SUZANNE: And very nice too!

THE COUNTESS: Are you going to let her go?

FIGARO: Of course not! I'll dress somebody else in Suzanne's clothes: when we surprise him at the rendezvous, how will he be able to get out of it?

SUZANNE: And who are you dressing up in my clothes?

FIGARO: Chérubin.

THE COUNTESS: He's gone.

FIGARO: Not if I know anything. Will you leave it to me?

SUZANNE: Since it's a question of intrigue we can.

FIGARO: Two, three, four threads at once – tangled and crossed into the bargain! I'm a courtier born. . . .

SUZANNE: They say it's a difficult trade.

FIGARO: Receive, take, ask again – that's the secret in so many words.

THE COUNTESS: He has so much confidence he ends by inspiring me with it!

FIGARO: That's the intention.

SUZANNE: You were saying –

FIGARO: That while His Lordship is away I'll send Chérubin to you. You arrange his hair and dress him up. I'll get hold of him and teach him his part and then – dance, Your Lordship! [*Exit* FIGARO.]

THE COUNTESS [*powder-box in hand*]: Heavens, Suzie, what a sight I am! This young man who's coming in . . .

SUZANNE: Your Ladyship doesn't mean to let him off?

THE COUNTESS [*lost in thought before her glass*]: I? You see how I'll scold him. . . .

SUZANNE: Let's make him sing his ballad. [*Puts it on the Countess's knee.*]

THE COUNTESS: My hair really is in a most dreadful state. . . .

SUZANNE: We only have two curls to do again. Your Ladyship will scold him all the better –

THE COUNTESS [*dreaming*]: What's that you say?
    [*Enter* CHÉRUBIN *with a disconsolate air.*]

SUZANNE: Come in, gallant officer! The ladies are at home.

CHÉRUBIN [*coming forward hesitatingly*]: Oh! How that word hurts me! It reminds me that I have to go away and leave a godmother who was so kind . . .

SUZANNE: And so beautiful!

CHÉRUBIN [*with a sigh*]: Yes, of course!

SUZANNE [*imitating him*]: Yes, of course! Poor little man with

his sly downcast eyes! Come on, pretty one, sing Her Ladyship your ballad.

THE COUNTESS [*opening it*]: About whom is it ... may one
ask?

SUZANNE: Look! How he blushes!

CHÉRUBIN: Is it wrong to ... to be in love?

SUZANNE [*putting her fist under his nose*]: I'll tell everything,
you wretch!

THE COUNTESS: There now – can he sing?

CHÉRUBIN: Ah, Madam! I'm so nervous. ...

SUZANNE [*laughing*]: There, there, diddums then! As soon as
Her Ladyship wants to hear it, we go all modest and shy.
I'll accompany you.

THE COUNTESS: Take my guitar.

[*She sits holding the manuscript to follow the music.* SUZANNE
*is behind the chair and reads the accompaniment over her Mis-
tress's shoulder. The page faces them, eyes downcast as in the
print after Vanloo called 'Conversation Espagnole'.*]

CHÉRUBIN [*to the tune* 'Marlbrough s'en va t'en Guerre']:

My steed was weary and slow
(Alas, but my heart is in pain)
Our heads alike hanging low
As we wandered over the plain.

As we wandered over the plain
(Alas, but my heart is in pain)
My tears I strove to restrain
As I rode with a loose-hanging rein.

As I rode with a loose-hanging rein
(Alas, but my heart is in pain)
The Queen passing by said, 'Pray tell me why
You ride with a tear in your eye.'

Why you ride with a tear in your eye
(Alas, but my heart is in pain)
I shall ne'er see my true love again
I shall ne'er see my true love again.

THE COUNTESS: Very artless and – quite moving . . . in its way. . . .

SUZANNE [*putting the guitar on a chair*]: Oh, yes, when it comes to sentiment this young man is . . . but have they told you, gallant Sir, how we mean to enliven the evening. We want to see first whether you can get my dress on. . . .

THE COUNTESS: I fear not.

SUZANNE [*measuring herself against him*]: He's about my height. Let's have the coat off first. [*Takes it off.*]

THE COUNTESS: Suppose someone were to come.

SUZANNE: We are doing nothing wrong. I'll go and shut the door. I want to see what we can do about his hair first. . . .

THE COUNTESS: There's a bonnet of mine on the table.

[SUZANNE *goes into closet off-stage.*]

Until the very moment the ball begins the Count won't know you are still at the castle. We'll explain to him afterwards that it was having to wait for your commission to be made out that suggested the idea to us. . . .

CHÉRUBIN [*showing it*]: Alas, Your Ladyship – I already have it here. Bazile handed it to me.

THE COUNTESS: So soon! They didn't mean to lose any time. [*She reads it.*] They were in such a hurry they forgot to put the seal on. [*She hands it back to him.*]

SUZANNE [*coming in with a large bonnet*]: What seal on what?

THE COUNTESS: On his commission.

SUZANNE: Already?

THE COUNTESS: That was what I said. Is that my bonnet?

SUZANNE [*sitting beside the Countess*]: It's the nicest one you have. [*Singing with pins in her mouth*]

> Turn and face me
> Dearest love . . .

[CHÉRUBIN *kneels down and she does his hair.*]

Madam – he looks charming.

THE COUNTESS: Make it look more girlish at the neck.

SUZANNE [*adjusting it*]: There! Just look at the little brat! Doesn't he make a pretty girl? I'm really quite jealous. [*Takes him by the chin.*] Wouldn't you like to be pretty like this?

THE COUNTESS: Silly! Tuck up the sleeve so that the under-sleeve shows better. [*She pushes it up.*] What's this on his wrist, a ribbon?

SUZANNE: And one of yours! I'm very pleased Your Ladyship has seen it. I told him I'd tell you. I'd have got it back if His Lordship hadn't come in when he did. I'm nearly as strong as he is.

THE COUNTESS: There's blood on it. [*She takes off the ribbon.*]

CHÉRUBIN [*ashamed*]: It happened this morning. Thinking I was leaving . . . I was arranging my horse's bit – he tossed his head and the point of the curb cut my wrist.

THE COUNTESS: But one would never use a ribbon to bandage . . .

SUZANNE: Particularly a stolen one . . . what is all this about curbs and bits and studs, anyway! I don't understand a word of it. . . . Oh! Look how white his arm is – like a girl's! It's whiter than mine. Just look, Your Ladyship!

[*The* COUNTESS *compares them.*]

THE COUNTESS [*crossly*]: You would do better to get me the sticking-plaster from my room.

[*The* COUNTESS *does not speak for a moment – her eyes are on the ribbon while* CHÉRUBIN's *eyes devour her.*]

As to the ribbon, Sir – the colour particularly suits me and I should have been very sorry to have lost it.

SUZANNE [*returning*]: How are you going to tie it up? [*Gives the Countess sticking-plaster and scissors.*]

THE COUNTESS: While you are looking for clothes for him take the ribbon out of another bonnet.

  [SUZANNE *goes out off-stage, taking with her Chérubin's cloak.*]

CHÉRUBIN [*eyes on ground, still kneeling*]: The one I had would soon have made it better.

THE COUNTESS: How? [*Offers the sticking-plaster.*] This will do more good.

CHÉRUBIN [*shyly*]: When a ribbon has been used to bind the hair or touched the skin of someone – some person . . .

THE COUNTESS [*sharply*]: Unknown – it acquires healing properties, eh? I wasn't aware of it! I'll keep the one which bound your arm just to try it. The first time one of my women cuts herself – we'll see what happens.

CHÉRUBIN [*sadly*]: You will keep it. And I shall go away.

THE COUNTESS: Not for ever.

CHÉRUBIN: I'm so unhappy.

THE COUNTESS [*moved*]: He's crying. It's all because of what that wicked Figaro said about soldiers.

CHÉRUBIN: Ah, would it were the moment he foretold! Were I but sure of dying here and now perchance my lips would venture . . .

THE COUNTESS [*interrupting him and drying his eyes with her handkerchief*]: There, there, child! What nonsense you do talk!

  [*Knock on door.*]

Who's that knocking?

THE COUNT [*outside*]: Why are you locked in?

THE COUNTESS: Heavens! My husband! [*To Chérubin*] You without your coat, your neck and arms all bare, alone here with me! Everything in disorder – and he'll have had the letter – Oh! and he so jealous!

THE COUNT: Are you not going to open?

THE COUNTESS: I'm ... I'm alone.

THE COUNT: Alone – then to whom are you talking?

THE COUNTESS [*desperately*]: You, of course.

CHÉRUBIN [*aside*]: After what happened yesterday and this morning he'll kill me on the spot.

[*He runs to the dressing-closet and pulls the door to behind him. The* COUNTESS *takes the key out and runs to open the door to the Count.*]

THE COUNTESS: Oh! How could we be so foolish!

THE COUNT [*a little severely*]: You don't usually lock yourself in.

THE COUNTESS [*ill at ease*]: I was sewing. Yes, I was doing some sewing with Suzanne. She's just gone through to her room, as I told you.

THE COUNT: You look worried.

THE COUNTESS: It's not surprising – not in the least – we were just talking about you, and, as I said, she's just gone. ...

THE COUNT: Talking about me, were you? I came back because I'm concerned about a letter that was put into my hands just as I was about to mount my horse. I don't believe a word of it but – all the same – I'm ... concerned.

THE COUNTESS: Why? What letter?

THE COUNT: The fact is, Madam, there are some pretty disreputable people about. I have been warned that someone might be endeavouring to see you today ... unknown to me.

THE COUNTESS: Then he'll have to get in here, whoever he may be. I don't intend to leave my room today.

THE COUNT: Even though Suzanne is getting married this evening?

THE COUNTESS: Not on any account. I'm not well.

THE COUNT: Fortunately the Doctor is here.

[*The* PAGE *knocks a chair over in the closet.*]
What's that noise?

THE COUNTESS: *What* noise?

THE COUNT: Someone knocked something over.

THE COUNTESS: I didn't hear anything.

THE COUNT: You must be terribly preoccupied.

THE COUNTESS: Preoccupied – with what?

THE COUNT: There is someone in that room, Madam.

THE COUNTESS: And – whom do you imagine it could be?

THE COUNT: That's what I'm asking you. I have only just come.

THE COUNTESS: It must be Suzanne – apparently she's looking for something.

THE COUNT: You said she'd gone to her room.

THE COUNTESS: She went out somewhere – in there or somewhere else. I don't know just where.

THE COUNT: If it's Suzanne why are you so concerned?

THE COUNTESS: Concerned about my maid?

THE COUNT: I don't know about your maid, but you are certainly concerned.

THE COUNTESS: What is certain, Sir, is that you are concerned about her – much more than I am.

THE COUNT: I'm so far concerned, Madam, that I want to see her immediately.

THE COUNTESS: I believe you often do so – but there's nothing in your suspicions.

[*Enter* SUZANNE *upstage with dresses.*]

THE COUNT: Then they'll be the more easily disposed of.
[*He looks towards the dressing-room and calls to Suzanne*] Come out, Suzie, come out!

[SUZANNE *stops near the door to the alcove upstage.*]

THE COUNTESS: She's practically undressed. Do you really

have to come disturbing us women like this? She was trying on some dresses I was giving her as a wedding present. She ran out when she heard you coming.

THE COUNT: If she doesn't want to be seen – she can at least make herself heard. [*Indicating the dressing-room*] Answer, Suzie, are you there?

[SUZANNE *upstage, goes into alcove and hides*.]

THE COUNTESS [*hurrying towards the dressing-room*]: Suzie, I forbid you to reply. [*To the Count*] Whoever heard of such outrageous behaviour!

THE COUNT [*moving towards the dressing-room*]: All right! If she won't answer I'll see her – dressed or undressed.

THE COUNTESS [*standing in front of him*]: I may not be able to prevent it elsewhere, but I should hope that here in my own room . . .

THE COUNT: I'll know who this mysterious Suzanne is. I suppose it's no use asking you for the key, but there's no difficulty in breaking the door in. Hello, there!

THE COUNTESS: Go on! Call your servants! Cause a public scandal! Make us the talk of the castle!

THE COUNT: Very well, Madam. I can manage myself – I'll just go and get what I need. [*He makes to go out and turns back.*] But so that everything remains as it is will you be good enough to come with me and avoid the scandal and gossip which you find so displeasing? You won't refuse me so simple a request?

THE COUNTESS [*troubled*]: Ah, Sir, who would think of refusing you anything?

THE COUNT: Ah, I was forgetting the door to the maid's quarters. I must lock that as well in order that you may be fully justified. [*He goes to the door upstage and takes the key.*]

THE COUNTESS [*aside*]: Heavens – what dreadful obstinacy!

THE COUNT [*rejoining her*]: Now that the room is secured may I offer you my arm? [*Raising his voice*] And as for

Suzanne in the dressing-room, she must be good enough to wait for me: should any harm come to her before my return –

THE COUNTESS: Really, Sir! This is too horrible!

[*The* COUNT *leads her off and locks the door behind him.*]

SUZANNE [*running out from the alcove to the door of the dressing-room*]: Open, Chérubin, open at once – it's Suzanne – open and come out!

CHÉRUBIN [*coming out*]: Ah, Suzie! What a dreadful business!

SUZANNE: Out you go! You haven't a moment to lose!

CHÉRUBIN: But how?

SUZANNE: I don't know, but you must.

CHÉRUBIN: Supposing there *isn*'t a way out?

SUZANNE: After what's just happened he'd murder you and it would be the end of all of us. Run and tell Figaro what's happened.

CHÉRUBIN: Perhaps it's not too big a drop into the garden. [*Runs to the window.*]

SUZANNE [*frightened*]: It's a whole storey. Impossible! Oh, my poor mistress! And my wedding! Oh Heavens!

CHÉRUBIN: It's over the kitchen garden – I might get away at the price of spoiling a few of his flower-beds.

SUZANNE [*holding him back*]: He'll kill himself!

CHÉRUBIN [*exalted*]: Into the flaming pit itself, Suzie, rather than any harm should come to her – a kiss for luck! [*He kisses her, runs to the window, and jumps out.*]

SUZANNE [*uttering a cry of fright*]: Ah! [*Falls into a chair: goes miserably to the window and looks out.*] Oh, he's already quite a distance away! The young scamp! As nimble as he's pretty! If he ever wants for women . . . I'd better take his place at once. [*Going into the dressing-room*] Now, Your High-ness, you can break the lock if you want to; Devil a word will I answer. [*Goes in.*]

THE COUNT [*entering, pincers in hand*]: Everything as I left it! Before you oblige me to break open the door, consider the consequences. Once again, will you open it?

THE COUNTESS: Ah, Sir! Whatever can induce you to destroy our relationship? Were it love that drove you to such fury I could excuse your immoderation. I could perhaps forget – if that were the reason – how offensive was your method of showing it. But can mere vanity drive a man of honour to such excesses?

THE COUNT: Love or vanity, you shall open the door or I'll . . .

THE COUNTESS: Do stop, Sir, if you please! Do you really believe I can be so wanting in self-respect?

THE COUNT: I'll believe anything you like, Madam, but I mean to see who's in the dressing-room.

THE COUNTESS [*alarmed*]: Very well, Sir. You *shall* see. Only listen a moment –

THE COUNT: Then it isn't Suzie?

THE COUNTESS [*timidly*]: At least it is someone – whom you can't be mistrustful of. . . . We were preparing a joke – an entirely innocent joke for this evening, and I assure you –

THE COUNT: Of what do you assure me?

THE COUNTESS: That we had no intention of offending you – he or I.

THE COUNT: So it is a man!

THE COUNTESS: A boy, Sir!

THE COUNT: Ha! And who is it?

THE COUNTESS: I hardly dare mention his name.

THE COUNT [*furious*]: I'll kill him.

THE COUNTESS: Great heavens!

THE COUNT: Speak then!

THE COUNTESS: Young – Chérubin –

THE COUNT: Chérubin! The impudent scoundrel! All my suspicions – in the letter – are justified.

THE COUNTESS [*joining her hands*]: Ah, Sir – please don't think –

THE COUNT [*stamping his foot – aside*]: This confounded page, I run across him everywhere. Come, Madam, open! You could have spared your emotion when you took leave of him this morning: had he gone when I commanded him you wouldn't have needed to resort to such deceit in your story about Suzanne: and he wouldn't have been so carefully concealed if there had been nothing wrong in it.

THE COUNTESS: He was afraid you would be angry if you saw him.

[*The* COUNT, *beside himself, hurries towards the dressing-room.*]

THE COUNT: Come out, you little wretch!

THE COUNTESS [*pushing him away*]: Ah, Sir, your anger gives me concern for his safety. Don't, please don't harbour unjust suspicions – don't let his disordered dress –

THE COUNT: His disordered dress!

THE COUNTESS: Alas, Sir! He was getting ready to dress as a woman – my bonnet on his head . . . in his shirt without his coat – neck open – arms bare . . . he was going to try on . . .

THE COUNT: And you were going to keep to your room – unworthy wife! Ay, you *shall* keep to it, and for a long time too! But first I'll punish the impudent scoundrel so that I shall never come across him anywhere any more!

THE COUNTESS [*throwing herself on her knees*]: Oh, My Lord! Spare the boy! I shall never forgive myself for having caused . . .

THE COUNT: Your concern for him aggravates his offence.

THE COUNTESS: He's not to blame – he was going away. It was I who recalled him. . . .

THE COUNT [*furious*]: Get up and begone! How dare you plead for him!

THE COUNTESS: All right, I will go, Sir. I *will* get up. I even give you the key of the room. But in the name of your love – for me –

THE COUNT: My love for you! Perfidious creature!

THE COUNTESS [*handing him the key*]: Promise that you will let the boy go unharmed. Then you may vent all your fury on me if I cannot convince you . . .

THE COUNT [*taking the key*]: I'll hear no more!

THE COUNTESS [*throwing herself on to couch*]: Heavens! It's the end of him!

THE COUNT [*opening door*]: Suzanne!

SUZANNE [*comes out laughing*]: 'I'll kill him! I'll kill him!' Kill him then, the wretched page!

THE COUNT [*aside*]: Ah! What a sell! [*Looking at the Countess, who is petrified with astonishment*] And you too – pretending to be astonished! But perhaps she's not alone. . . . [*Goes in.*]

SUZANNE [*running to her mistress*]: Pull yourself together, Mistress. He's far enough away. He jumped out.

THE COUNTESS: Ah, Suzie! I shall never survive it!

[*The* COUNT *comes out of the dressing-room bewildered. After a short silence*]

THE COUNT: There's nobody there. I was entirely wrong. Madam, you are quite an actress.

SUZANNE [*gaily*]: And I, My Lord?

[*The* COUNTESS, *her handkerchief to her mouth while she recovers her composure, says nothing.*]

THE COUNT: So you were pleased to joke, Madam!

THE COUNTESS [*recovering a little*]: And why not, Sir?

THE COUNT: A pretty dreadful sort of joke! What's the point of it, I ask you?

THE COUNTESS: Do your follies deserve any sympathy?

THE COUNT: Follies you call them – where my honour is involved?

THE COUNTESS [*gradually becoming more assured*]: Did I marry you to be delivered over to perpetual neglect and jealousy – such as only you dare justify –

THE COUNT: Ah, Madam! It was not intentional.

SUZANNE: Her ladyship need only have let you call the servants –

THE COUNT: True. I have indeed reason to be ashamed. Forgive me, I'm not quite myself. . . .

SUZANNE: You must admit, My Lord, that you did deserve it – a little.

THE COUNT: But why didn't you come out when I called – you wretch!

SUZANNE: I was getting dressed, pinning myself together again, and besides, Her Ladyship had told me not to – and she did quite right.

THE COUNT: Why don't you help me to gain her forgiveness instead of harping on my errors.

THE COUNTESS: No, Sir! An outrage of this kind cannot be passed over. . . . I shall retire into a convent. I can see that it is more than time that I did so.

THE COUNT: And could you do so – without some regrets?

SUZANNE: It *would* be a sad day for everyone, I'm sure.

THE COUNTESS: Ah, would it were so, Suzie! Better regrets than the humiliation of forgiving him. He has offended me too deeply.

THE COUNT: Rosine!

THE COUNTESS: I'm no longer the Rosine whom you once wooed so assiduously. I'm the Countess Almaviva, the sad and neglected wife whom you no longer love.

SUZANNE: Madam!

THE COUNT [*in supplication*]: For pity's sake . . .

THE COUNTESS: You had none for me.

THE COUNT: It was the letter that made my blood boil.

THE COUNTESS: I wasn't responsible for that.

THE COUNT: But you knew of it?

THE COUNTESS: It was that stupid Figaro.

THE COUNT: *He* was in it?

THE COUNTESS: He handed it to Bazile.

THE COUNT: Who said he had it from a peasant. Oh, treacherous music master! You shall pay for the whole lot!

THE COUNTESS: You ask forgiveness for yourself, but you deny it to others. That's men exactly! Supposing I *were* to grant my forgiveness on the grounds that you were provoked by the letter – it would have to be a general pardon.

THE COUNT: With all my heart – but however can I make amends for so heinous a fault?

THE COUNTESS: The fault was on both sides.

THE COUNT: Ah, no! Say it was mine only! What's beyond my comprehension is how women can so quickly and convincingly assume the air and tone that the circumstances require. You blushed; you wept; you seemed embarrassed. Upon my word, you still do!

THE COUNTESS [*forcing herself to smile*]: I blushed – from resentment at your suspicions. But men are not sufficiently sensitive to distinguish between righteous indignation – and guilty embarrassment.

THE COUNT [*smiling*]: And the page in a state of disorder – undressed – almost naked?

THE COUNTESS: Is before you now. Aren't you pleased that you have found *her* rather than the person you expected to find? You don't usually show any objection to meeting her!

THE COUNT [*laughing*]: And the entreaties and feigned tears?

THE COUNTESS: You make me laugh, but it's no laughing matter.

THE COUNT: We men think we know something about dissimulation, but we are only children. It's you, you, Madam, whom the King should be sending as his Ambassador to

London. How women must study the art of controlling their demeanour to succeed in such a degree!

THE COUNTESS: You men drive us to it.

SUZANNE: Regard us as prisoners on parole and you'll see whether we can be trusted.

THE COUNTESS: Let us leave it at that! I may have gone too far, but my forbearance under such grave provocation ought at least to ensure me yours.

THE COUNT: But will you confirm that you forgive me?

THE COUNTESS: Did I ever say that I would, Suzie?

SUZANNE: I didn't hear it, Your Ladyship.

THE COUNT: Ah, then – won't you say it now?

THE COUNTESS: Do you deserve it, ungrateful man?

THE COUNT: Has my repentance not earned it?

SUZANNE: Imagining there was a man in Her Ladyship's dressing-room!

THE COUNT: She has punished me severely!

SUZANNE: Not believing her when she said it was her maid!

THE COUNT: Are you really implacable, Rosine?

THE COUNTESS: Ah, Suzie! How weak I am! What an example I set you. [*Giving the Count her hand*] No one will believe in a woman's resentment any more.

SUZANNE: Well! Don't we always have to come to this with them in the end?

[*The* COUNT *kisses his wife's hand ardently. Enter* FIGARO *out of breath.*]

FIGARO: I heard Your Ladyship was unwell. . . . I came as quickly as I could. I'm delighted to see it was nothing.

THE COUNT [*harshly*]: You are very attentive!

FIGARO: It's my duty, Sir. But, since apparently there's nothing in it, may I say, Sir, that all the young men and women in your service are below with violins and pipes and waiting to accompany me – as soon as you will permit me – to conduct my bride to . . .

THE COUNT: And who will stay and look after the Countess at the castle?

FIGARO: Stay and look after her? She isn't ill?

THE COUNT: No, but what about the man who is coming to visit her?

FIGARO: What man?

THE COUNT: The man in the letter you gave to Bazile!

FIGARO: Who said I did?

THE COUNT: If no one else had told me, you dog, your own face would accuse you and prove you a liar.

FIGARO: In that case my face must be lying. I'm not.

SUZANNE: My poor, dear Figaro, don't waste words in denying. We have told everything.

FIGARO: And what have you told? What do you take me for? A Bazile?

SUZANNE: We told how you wrote the letter so that when His Lordship came in he would believe that the page was in the dressing-room where I was hiding.

THE COUNT: And what do you say to that?

THE COUNTESS: There's nothing to hide now, Figaro, the joke's over.

FIGARO [*trying to make it out*]: The joke ... is over?

THE COUNT: Yes – all over. What do you say to that, eh?

FIGARO: What do I say? That I wish I could say the same for my marriage, and if you will give your command . . .

THE COUNT: You admit then about the letter. . . .

FIGARO: Since Her Ladyship wants it that way and it's what Suzie wants and what you want yourself, then I suppose it must be what I want too. But if I were in your place, My Lord, I really wouldn't believe a word of it.

THE COUNT: You still go on lying in the teeth of the evidence. I shall end by getting annoyed.

THE COUNTESS [*laughing*]: Poor man! Must you really insist that he tells the truth for once?

FIGARO [*aside to Suzanne*]: I warned him of his danger. I couldn't be expected to do otherwise?

SUZANNE [*aside*]: Did you see the page?

FIGARO [*aside*]: Still a bit shaken.

SUZANNE [*aside*]: Oh! Poor boy!

THE COUNTESS: Come, My Lord, they are longing to be united: their impatience is natural: let us go down to the ceremony.

THE COUNT [*aside*]: And Marceline . . . Marceline . . . [*to the others*] I would just like to change for the occasion.

THE COUNTESS: For our own servants? I haven't.

[*Enter* ANTONIO *with a broken wallflower pot.*]

ANTONIO: My Lord! My Lord!

THE COUNT: Well, Antonio, what do you want?

ANTONIO: I want bars on the widows that open on to my flower-beds. They chuck all sorts of things down. They've just thrown a man out.

THE COUNT: Out of these windows?

ANTONIO: Look what they've done to my wallflowers!

SUZANNE [*aside*]: Look out, Figaro! Look out!

FIGARO: My Lord! He's been drunk all the morning.

ANTONIO: That's where you are wrong! It's a hangover from yesterday. See how they jump to herroneous conclusions!

THE COUNT [*fiercely*]: Where is this man? Where is he?

ANTONIO: Where is he?

THE COUNT: Yes.

ANTONIO: That's just what I want to know. It's what I have been trying to find out. I'm Your Lordship's servant – the only fellow that cares anything about your garden: a man comes tumbling into it . . . and you understand . . . my reputation's involved. . . .

SUZANNE [*low, to Figaro*]: Get him off the subject. . . .

FIGARO: So you *will* keep on drinking?

ANTONIO: I should go mad if I didn't.

THE COUNTESS: But why drink so much?

ANTONIO: That's all that distinguishes us from the beasts, Madam – drinking when we aren't thirsty and making love whenever we feel like it. . . .

THE COUNT: Give me an answer, now, or I shall turn you away.

ANTONIO: And do you think I should go?

THE COUNT: What do you mean?

ANTONIO [*touching his forehead*]: If you haven't enough up here to know when to keep a good servant, I'm not so soft as to get rid of a good master.

THE COUNT [*shaking him*]: You said someone had thrown a man out of this window.

ANTONIO: That's it, Your Excellency. Just now, in a white shirt he was, and he ran off, egad, like . . .

THE COUNT [*impatiently*]: And then?

ANTONIO: I would have run after him, but I had given myself such a clout against the gate that I couldn't lift a finger. . . .

THE COUNT: Anyway you'd recognize the fellow?

ANTONIO: Ay, that I would – if I had had a good look at him.

SUZANNE [*whispering to Figaro*]: He didn't see who it was.

FIGARO: What a fuss about a plant pot. How much do you want for your wallflower, you old misery? There's no point in looking for him, My Lord. I was the man who jumped out.

THE COUNT: You?

ANTONIO: 'How much do you want, you old misery!' You've grown a bit since then. You looked a deal shorter and slimmer to me.

FIGARO: Of course – one crouches in jumping.

ANTONIO: I would have said it was more like . . . that whippersnapper of a page.

THE COUNT: Chérubin, you mean?

FIGARO: Yes, with his horse as well, I suppose – come back from the gates of Seville on purpose to do it.

ANTONIO: No, no. I didn't say that. I didn't see no horses jump out, or I'd have said so.

THE COUNT: Heaven grant me patience!

FIGARO: I was in the bedroom – in a white shirt. . . . It was so hot. I was waiting for Suzie when I heard Your Lordship's voice – and a great to-do . . . and, I don't quite know why – but I took fright because of the letter – I must admit I was foolish. I jumped down into the flower-bed. I twisted my ankle a bit. [*Rubs it.*]

ANTONIO: Well if it were you, then I ought to give you this bit of paper that dropped out of your jacket as you fell.

THE COUNT [*snatching it*]: Give it me. [*Opens it and rolls it up again.*]

FIGARO [*aside*]: Caught!

THE COUNT: I suppose the fright won't have made you forget what's in the letter or how it came to be in your pocket?

FIGARO [*embarrassed, feeling in his pockets*]: Of course not . . . but I have so many – they are all to reply to . . . [*Looks at one piece of paper.*] What's this, for example? Ah, a letter from Marceline – four pages of it: very nice too – and what's this? Could it be the petition from that unfortunate poacher who's in jail? No, that's here. I had the inventory of the palace furniture in the other pocket. . . .

[*The* COUNT *again opens the paper he is holding.*]

THE COUNTESS [*whispers to Suzanne*]: Heavens, Suzie! It's his officer's warrant.

SUZANNE [*to Figaro*]: All's lost – it's the warrant for his commission.

THE COUNT [*refolding the paper*]: Can't you guess – and you a man of so many resources?

ANTONIO [*approaching Figaro*]: His Lordship says can't you guess?

FIGARO: Don't come shoving into me, you clown!

THE COUNT: You don't recall what it is, then?

FIGARO: Oh! Goodness me! It will be the commission of that unfortunate boy. He gave it to me, and I forgot to let him have it back! Oh dear! How stupid of me! What will he do without it? I must run and . . .

THE COUNT: And why should he have given it to you?

FIGARO [*in difficulties*]: He wanted me to do . . . something with it . . .

THE COUNT [*looking at it*]: There's nothing omitted.

THE COUNTESS [*low to Suzanne*]: The seal –

SUZANNE [*low to Figaro*]: The seal's missing.

THE COUNT [*to Figaro*]: You don't reply.

FIGARO: It was . . . the fact is . . . there was something missing – he said it was the custom . . . to . . .

THE COUNT: Custom? What custom? The custom to what?

FIGARO: To seal it with your seal . . . Of course it may not have been worth the trouble. . . .

THE COUNT [*opening the scroll again and crumpling it up angrily*]: All right! It's evident I'm to know nothing! [*Aside*] This fellow Figaro is at the bottom of everything. If only I could get my own back! [*Makes to go.*]

FIGARO [*interrupting*]: Are you going without giving the authority for my marriage?

[*Enter* MARCELINE, BAZILE, *servants, and tenants.*]

MARCELINE: Don't give the authority, My Lord! Before you show him any favours you must do justice between us. He has obligations to me.

THE COUNT [*aside*]: Here's my chance of revenge!

FIGARO: Obligations! What sort of obligations? Explain yourself.

MARCELINE: I'll explain myself, you scoundrel!

[*The* COUNTESS *sits down.* SUZANNE *stands behind her.*]

THE COUNT: What is it all about, Marceline?

MARCELINE: A promise of marriage.

FIGARO: A receipt for money lent, nothing more.

MARCELINE: On condition that he marries me. You are a great nobleman ... Chief Justice of the province ...

THE COUNT: Present yourself before the Court ... there I do justice to each and all.

BAZILE [*pointing to Marceline*]: In that case will Your Highness permit me to establish my claims on Marceline?

THE COUNT [*aside*]: Ah! There's my rascally friend of the letter.

FIGARO: Another fool of the same sort.

THE COUNT [*to Bazile – annoyed*]: Your claims! Your claims! You do well to talk of your claims before me, you blockhead of blockheads!

ANTONIO [*clapping his hands*]: Got him first time! That's him to a T.

THE COUNT: Marceline. Everything must be held up pending examination of your claims. It will be held publicly in the Great Hall. My good Bazile, trusty and reliable agent that you are, you can go into the town and find the members of the Bench.

BAZILE: For *his* case?

THE COUNT: And you can also bring along the peasant who gave you the letter.

BAZILE: How do I know him?

THE COUNT: Do you refuse?

BAZILE: I didn't come to the castle to run errands.

THE COUNT: Then what did you come for?

BAZILE: As village organist, teacher of the harpsichord to Her Ladyship, of singing to her ladies, and of the mandoline to the pages. Apart from that my major responsibility is to entertain Your Lordship's guests with my guitar whenever it pleases Your Highness to ask for it.

GRIPE-SOLEIL [*stepping forward*]: I'll go, My Lord, as it please you.

THE COUNT: Who are you and what is your job?

GRIPE-SOLEIL: Gripe-Soleil, Your Lordship. I be the herd boy for the goats and I be here for the fireworks today. I be on holiday from the herd and I know where all that made legal lot do hang out.

THE COUNT: Your zeal pleases me. Off you go! As for you – [*to Bazile*] accompany the gentleman and play the guitar to him on the way. He's one of my guests.

GRIPE-SOLEIL [*delighted*]: What, I be one?

[SUZANNE *restrains him, indicating that the Countess is present.*]

BAZILE [*amazed*]: I am to go with Gripe-Soleil and play . . .

THE COUNT: It's what you are here for. Off you go or I sack you. [*He goes out.*]

BAZILE [*to himself*]: I'm not going to quarrel with the kettle – since I'm only . . .

FIGARO: A mug!

BAZILE [*aside*]: I'll go and make sure of my own marriage with Marceline instead of helping at theirs. [*To Figaro*] Take my advice – don't settle anything until I come back. [*Picks up the guitar from the armchair upstage.*]

FIGARO [*following him*]: 'Don't settle anything!' Be off! I'm not worried – not even if you *never* come back. You don't seem to be singing. Shall I start you off? Come on! Cheer up! We'll have a song for the bride.

[*He leads the procession off in a* seguidilla; BAZILE *accompanies him and everyone joins in.*]

> Rather than riches
> I choose goodness – which is
> Whose?
> Why Sue – Sue – Suzie's
> Suzie's
> Suzie's . . .

[*They go off dancing and the sound of their singing dies away.*]

THE COUNTESS: Well, Suzanne, you see what a mess that foolish man of yours has got me into with his letter.

SUZANNE: Ah, Madam, if you could have seen your own face when I slipped out of the dressing-room! First it went white as a sheet, but it was only a passing moment, and then how you blushed! How you blushed!

THE COUNTESS: And he really jumped out of the window?

SUZANNE: Without hesitation, the dear boy! As light as a feather. . . .

THE COUNTESS: And that fatal gardener! I thought I should have died! I couldn't think of a thing.

SUZANNE: On the contrary, Madam – it was then that I saw how moving in high society teaches a lady to tell fibs without showing it at all.

THE COUNTESS: And do you think the Count was taken in? Suppose he were to find the boy was still at the castle.

SUZANNE: I'll tell him to keep so well hidden that . . .

THE COUNTESS: He must go. After what has just happened, you'll understand that I'm not anxious to send him to the rendezvous in the garden in place of you.

SUZANNE: And I'm certainly not going either. Now my marriage is again . . .

THE COUNTESS [*rising*]: Wait . . . instead of sending you or someone else – suppose I went myself.

SUZANNE: You, Madam?

THE COUNTESS: No one else need run any risk . . . the Count wouldn't be able to deny it . . . having punished his jealousy and proved his unfaithfulness it would be . . . Come, we have been lucky once – I'm tempted to try again. Let him know at once that you'll be in the garden. But above all, let no one else know.

SUZANNE: What about Figaro –

THE COUNTESS: No, he would want to put his own oar in.

... My mask and my cane and I'll go on to the terrace and think about it.

[SUZANNE *goes into dressing-room.*]

It's quite audacious – my little scheme. [*Turning round.*] Oh, my ribbon, my dear little ribbon! I had forgotten you! [*She rolls it up.*] I won't part with you, you shall remind me of the incident when the poor child – Ah, My Lord the Count! What have you done? And what am I doing now?

[*Enter* SUZANNE. *The* COUNTESS *slips the ribbon into her bosom.*]

SUZANNE: Here's the cane and your mask.

THE COUNTESS: Remember. I forbid you to say a word to Figaro.

SUZANNE: Madam, it's a delightful scheme. I've just been thinking about it. It fits everything together, rounds it all off, and brings everything to a conclusion – and whatever happens my marriage is certain now.

[*She kisses the Countess's hand and they go out.*]

*

During the Interval attendants arrange the Great Hall: they bring in benches for the lawyers which are placed to either side but leaving free passage behind. Mid-stage they put a platform with two steps and set the Count's chair on it. Downstage they set a table for the clerk and his stool beside it and seats for Brid'oison and the other judges on either side of the Count.

ACT THREE

SCENE: *A room in the castle known as the Throne Room, which serves as an audience chamber: on one side a canopy over a portrait of the King.*

[*Enter the* COUNT *and* PEDRILLO *in riding attire holding a sealed packet.*]

THE COUNT [*sharply*]: You understand?

PEDRILLO: Yes, Your Excellency. [*Goes out.*]

THE COUNT: Pedrillo!

PEDRILLO [*returning*]: Excellency?

THE COUNT: No one has seen you?

PEDRILLO: Not a soul.

THE COUNT: Take the Arab.

PEDRILLO: He's at the gate, saddled and ready.

THE COUNT: Right! Straight to Seville, then.

PEDRILLO: Only three leagues and a good road.

THE COUNT: When you get there find if the page has arrived.

PEDRILLO: At the house.

THE COUNT: Yes – and what's more, find out how long he's been there!

PEDRILLO: I understand.

THE COUNT: Deliver him his commission and come back at once.

PEDRILLO: And if he's not there?

THE COUNT: Come back all the quicker – and let me know Off you go!

[*Exit* PEDRILLO.]

THE COUNT: I made a mistake in sending Bazile away. Temper is no help at all. The note sent by him warning me of a plot against the Countess – the maid shut in the dressing-room when I arrived – her Mistress in a state of alarm – real or feigned – a man jumping out of the window and the other fellow admitting – or pretending it was he. . . . I don't get the thread of it all . . . there's something not clear somewhere . . . the liberties some of my people are taking – not that it matters unduly among such people – but the Countess? Suppose some fellow were to attempt . . . what am I talking about . . .? The truth is that when one lets one's temper run away with one even the best-regulated imagination may become disordered. She was just having a joke . . . the suppressed laughter, the joy she could hardly repress – after all she knows what is due to herself! Then there's my honour – how the Deuce does that stand? On the other hand, where am I myself getting to? Has that chit Suzanne given me away? She's not married to him yet. How do I come to be involved in this preposterous entanglement? A score of times I've wanted to give it up. . . . It just shows where not knowing one's own mind leads one . . . If it were just a straightforward question I shouldn't have anything like the desire for her that I have. This fellow Figaro always keeps one waiting. I must sound him carefully . . . [FIGARO *appears upstage – he stops*] . . . and find out by some means whether or not he knows what I feel about Suzanne.

FIGARO [*aside*]: Now for it!

THE COUNT [*aside*]: If she's said a single word to him –

FIGARO [*aside*]: I'm under suspicion.

THE COUNT [*aside*]: I'll make him marry the old woman.

FIGARO [*aside*]: Master Bazile's fancy, eh?

THE COUNT [*aside*]: And then we'll see what can be done with the girl.

FIGARO [*aside*]: My wife, if you don't mind.

THE COUNT [*turning round*]: Ah, what's that?

FIGARO: Me – you sent for me.

THE COUNT: And what were you saying?

FIGARO: I said nothing.

THE COUNT: 'My wife, if you don't mind.'

FIGARO: It was the end of a sentence. I was saying to someone else, 'Go tell my wife, if you don't mind.'

THE COUNT [*walking up and down*]: His *wife*! And may I inquire what business could be detaining you, Sir, when I had summoned you here?

FIGARO [*pretending to dust his clothes*]: I got myself dirty when I fell into those flower-beds. I've been changing.

THE COUNT: Does that take an hour?

FIGARO: It takes a while.

THE COUNT: The servants in this house take longer to dress than their masters.

FIGARO: Because they have no servants to assist them.

THE COUNT: I still don't understand what made you take such a foolish risk as to throw yourself –

FIGARO: Risk! Anyone might think I'd been buried alive!

THE COUNT: Don't try to prevaricate with me, Sir! You understand perfectly well that I'm not interested in the risk that you took but in your reason for taking it.

FIGARO: You arrive in a state of fury as a result of false information – raging like a torrent in the Sierra Morena – you are looking for a man, and a man you mean to have, or you'll force the lock or break down the doors. I just happened to be there and who was to know, in the state you were in, what . . .

THE COUNT: You could have escaped down the stairs.

FIGARO: And let you catch me in the passage?

THE COUNT [*furious*]: In the passage? [*Aside*] I'm losing my self-control. . . . I shan't get the information I want.

FIGARO [*aside*]: Careful! We must play our cards cautiously.

THE COUNT [*recovering himself*]: That wasn't what I wanted to talk about. We'll leave it. I was thinking – yes – I had some

idea of taking you with me to London as my courier but –
on reflection . . .

FIGARO: Your Lordship has changed his mind.

THE COUNT: In the first place you don't know any English.

FIGARO: I can say 'God damn!'

THE COUNT: I don't understand.

FIGARO: I said I can say 'God damn!'

THE COUNT: Well? And what about it?

FIGARO: Why! English is a devilish fine language. You can
get along with so little of it..If you can say 'God damn!' you
needn't want for anything anywhere in England. Suppose
you fancy a nice chicken, you go into a tavern and just do
like this to the waiter [*imitating a spit*]. 'God damn!' They
bring you a round of salt beef and no bread. It's amazing!
You feel like a bottle of good burgundy or claret, then you
just do so [*gesture of drawing a cork*]. 'God damn!' In they
come with a foaming tankard of beer. It's marvellous! Perhaps you meet some pretty wench coming mincing along,
eyes on the ground, elbows well back, hips lightly swing-
ing – you give her a friendly chuck under the chin. 'God
damn!' She lands you one that makes you wonder what hit
you! Which shows that she understands perfectly well. It's
true that the English put in a few other words here and
there in conversation but obviously 'God damn!' is the
basis of the language. So, if Your Highness has no other
reason for leaving me in Spain –

THE COUNT [*aside*]: He wants to come to London. She hasn't
said anything.

FIGARO [*aside*]: He thinks I know nothing. I'll play him at
his own game for a while.

THE COUNT: What made the Countess play such a trick on
me?

FIGARO: Upon my word, you know better than I do, My
Lord.

THE COUNT: I anticipate her every wish. I heap gifts upon her.

FIGARO: You give her presents, but you are unfaithful to her. Are we ever grateful for superfluities from those who deprive us of necessities?

THE COUNT: There was a time – when you told me everything. . . .

FIGARO: I'm hiding nothing from you now.

THE COUNT: How much has the Countess given you for your support in this pretty business?

FIGARO: How much did you give me for getting her out of the hands of the Doctor? Come, Your Excellency, don't let us humiliate a man who does us good service for fear of making him a bad valet.

THE COUNT: Why has there always to be some ambiguity in your behaviour?

FIGARO: Because you are always on the look-out for it.

THE COUNT: A detestable reputation!

FIGARO: And suppose I were better than my reputation? Are there many noblemen who could say as much?

THE COUNT: How many times have I seen you on the road to fortune and yet never getting there?

FIGARO: Think of the mob there is in these days all intent on setting the pace, hurrying, pushing, elbowing, trampling each other down, every man for himself and the Devil take the hindmost! That's how it is and for my part I've given it up.

THE COUNT: Given up your ambitions? [*Aside*] That's something new.

FIGARO [*aside*]: My turn now. [*To the Count*] Your Excellency was good enough to bestow on me the stewardship of the castle and a very pleasant existence it is. It's true that I miss the satisfactions of the bringer of exciting news, but, on the other hand, I shall dwell happily with my wife in the heart of Andalusia.

THE COUNT: What's to stop you taking her with you to London?

FIGARO: I should have to leave her so often I might find it tiresome.

THE COUNT: But with your brains and character you could hope for advancement in the service.

FIGARO: Brains a means to advancement! Your Highness is pleased to make fun of me. Mediocrity and subservience – those are the qualities one needs. Given them a man can get anywhere.

THE COUNT: You only need to study the art of politics a little under my direction.

FIGARO: I know it already.

THE COUNT: Like English, eh? . . . the basis of the language?

FIGARO: Yes – if it's anything to be proud of. To pretend not to know what one does know and know what one doesn't, to hear what one doesn't understand and not hear what one does, above all to promise beyond one's abilities; to make a great secret of hiding what isn't there; to withdraw to one's privacy and employ it in sharpening pens, appearing profound when one is really empty and dull, to play a part well or badly, to encourage spies and reward traitors, to tamper with seals, intercept letters, and endeavour to compensate for poverty of means by exaggerating the importance of one's ends – that's all there is in politics or I'm sadly mistaken.

THE COUNT: Oh, but what you are defining is intrigue.

FIGARO: Policy, intrigue – as you will! To my mind they are pretty much of a muchness. Let them meddle with them who want to. 'For I prefer my dearie oh!' as the old song says.

THE COUNT [aside]: He means to stay at home! I understand. Suzanne has given me away.

FIGARO [aside]: I'm paying him back in his own coin. Let him make what he can of that one!

THE COUNT: And so you hope to win your case against Marceline?

FIGARO: Will you make it a crime for me to refuse an old maid when Your Excellency permits himself to do us out of the young ones?

THE COUNT [*laughingly*]: On the Bench a magistrate puts his own interest aside and looks only to the provisions of the statute.

FIGARO: Indulgent to the strong, severe on the weak!

THE COUNT: Do you think I'm joking?

FIGARO: Ah! Who knows, My Lord! *Tempo e galant'uomo* as they say in Italian: time will show in the end who means harm and who doesn't.

THE COUNT [*aside*]: I see that he's heard everything. He shall marry the duenna.

FIGARO [*aside*]: He's been trying me out. What does he know?

[*Enter lackey.*]

LACKEY [*announcing*]: Don Guzman Brid'oison.

THE COUNT: Brid'oison?

FIGARO: Oh! Of course. The judge, your colleague and assessor.

[*For a moment* FIGARO *watches the Count, who is lost in thought.*]

THE COUNT: Send him in.

[*Exit lackey.*]

FIGARO: Is that all Your Excellency requires?

THE COUNT: What? Oh, yes. Arrange the room for the hearing.

FIGARO: What more is needed? The big armchair is for you, the others for your colleagues on the Bench, stool for the clerk, benches for the lawyers, the front of the hall for the gentry, and the rabble behind. I'll go and send away the cleaners. [*Exit.*]

THE COUNT: The rascal embarrasses me. Give him half a chance in discussion, he gets you in his grip and you are helpless. Scoundrels both of them! In league to take advantage of me! You can be friends – lovers – what you like to each other, I don't mind, but husband and wife –

[*Enter* SUZANNE, *out of breath.*]

SUZANNE: My Lord – Oh, beg pardon!

THE COUNT [*ironically*]: What is it, young lady?

SUZANNE: You are angry!

THE COUNT: You were wanting something, apparently.

SUZANNE [*shyly*]: The Mistress has the vapours. I was coming to ask you to lend us your smelling-salts. I'll return them immediately.

THE COUNT [*handing her the phial*]: Keep them for yourself. No doubt you'll soon find them useful.

SUZANNE: Do you imagine that women of my class have the vapours? It's a genteel malady. They only catch it in drawing-rooms.

THE COUNT: A loving bride and she's losing her young man. . . .

SUZANNE: But by paying Marceline with the dowry that you promised. . . .

THE COUNT: *I* promised?

SUZANNE [*lowering her gaze*]: My Lord, I thought I heard so.

THE COUNT: Ay! – if only you *would* hear me. . . .

SUZANNE [*eyes on the ground*]: Is it not my duty to listen to Your Lordship?

THE COUNT: Then why, cruel child, didn't you say so before?

SUZANNE: Is it ever too late for the truth?

THE COUNT: Will you be in the garden this evening?

SUZANNE: Don't I walk there every evening?

THE COUNT: Why were you so obstinate this morning?

SUZANNE: This morning – with the page behind the chair?

THE COUNT: She's quite right. I had forgotten. But why this persistent refusal when Bazile, on my behalf . . .

SUZANNE: What need of a Bazile?

THE COUNT: She's right again. But there's a certain Figaro to whom I fear you may have told things?

SUZANNE: Why, of course! I tell him everything – except what he ought not to know.

THE COUNT: Charming! And you promise me? If you go back on your word, let us be clear, my dear: no rendezvous no dowry – no dowry no marriage.

SUZANNE [*curtseying*]: But no marriage also means no *Droit de Seigneur*, My Lord!

THE COUNT: Where does she pick it all up? Upon my word I shall dote on her! But your Mistress is waiting for the phial. . . .

SUZANNE [*laughing and handing it back*]: I had to have some excuse to talk to you. . . .

THE COUNT [*trying to kiss her*]: Delicious creature!

SUZANNE [*evading him*]: Someone is coming.

THE COUNT [*aside*]: She's mine. [*Goes off.*]

SUZANNE: I must go and tell Her Ladyship.
  [*Enter* FIGARO.]

FIGARO: Suzanne. Where are you running off to . . . after parting from His Lordship?

SUZANNE: Go to Court now if you wish. You have just won your case. . . .

FIGARO [*following*]: Ah but . . . tell me . . . [*Exit.*]
  [*Enter the* COUNT.]

THE COUNT: 'You have just won your case!' What a beautiful trap I was walking into there! I'll punish you both for that, my imprudent friends! A just verdict . . . very just. . . . But suppose he *were* to pay the duenna – but what could he pay with? If he were to pay . . . Ah ha! Haven't I the proud Antonio whose lofty pride scorns the nonentity of a

Figaro for his niece – I'll encourage that idea and – why not? In the vast field of intrigue one must contrive to cultivate everything, even the vanity of an old fool. [*He calls*] Antonio! [*Goes off.*]

[*Enter* BRID'OISON, MARCELINE, *and* BARTHOLO.]

MARCELINE: Sir, please listen to my case.

BRID'OISON [*wearing his gown, stammering slightly*]: Very well, let's hear what you have to say.

BARTHOLO: It's a question of a promise of marriage . . .

MARCELINE: Along with a loan of money . . .

BRID'OISON: I follow – the usual consequences *et cetera.*

MARCELINE: No, Sir. No consequences – no *et cetera.*

BRID'OISON: I follow – have you got the money?

MARCELINE: No, Sir, I was the lender. . . .

BRID'OISON: I follow – you are wanting your money back.

MARCELINE: No, Sir, I want him to marry me.

BRID'OISON: Ah! Now I do follow – and does *he* want to marry you?

MARCELINE: No, Sir. That's what the case is about.

BRID'OISON: Do you think I don't f-follow that?

MARCELINE: No, Sir. [*To Bartholo*] Where are we? [*To Brid'oison*] What! Are you going to try the case?

BRID'OISON: What do you think I purchased the office for?

MARCELINE [*sighing*]: It's a great abuse – the sale of offices.

BRID'OISON: Yes, it would be better if we could get them for nothing. Whom are you suing?

[*Enter* FIGARO *rubbing his hands.*]

MARCELINE [*pointing to him*]: This wicked man, Sir.

FIGARO [*gaily to Marceline*]: I'm embarrassing you perhaps? [*To Brid'oison*] His Lordship will be here in a moment, Sir.

BRID'OISON: I've seen this fellow somewhere before.

FIGARO: In Seville, Sir. I was in your wife's service.

BRID'OISON: When was th-that?

FIGARO: Rather less than a year before the birth of your son,

Sir. The younger one, and a very handsome child too, if I may say so. . . .

BRID'OISON: He's the best looking one of the family. I understand you are up to your tricks again. . . .

FIGARO: You are too kind, Sir . . . it's a trifling matter.

BRID'OISON: A promise of marriage. Ah – poor simpleton!

FIGARO: Sir . . .

BRID'OISON: Has the young man seen my clerk?

FIGARO: You mean Doublemain? . . . the clerk of the Court?

BRID'OISON: Yes, he's got a finger in every pie.

FIGARO: Finger. Both hands if I know anything! Oh, yes, I've seen him about the depositions and the supplementary pleadings – all the usual procedure.

BRID'OISON: We have to comply with the forms. . . .

FIGARO: Oh, of course! Cases begin with the litigants but we all know it's the forms that enable lawyers to live.

BRID'OISON: This young man isn't as green as I thought. All right, friend, since you know a thing or two about the job we'll look after your interests.

FIGARO: Sir, I rely on your integrity even though you are one of our judges.

BRID'OISON: What's that? Oh, yes, I'm a judge. But if you owe money and won't pay . . .

FIGARO: Then you see, Sir, it's just as if it never was owing.

BRID'OISON: Quite! Hey! What's that he said?

[*Enter Usher preceding Court.*]

USHER: Gentlemen – His Lordship!

THE COUNT: Fully robed, Master Brid'oison! This is only a domestic matter. Ordinary dress would have been good enough here.

BRID'OISON: You are too good, Your Lordship, but I never go without it – you see it's a part of the forms. A man may laugh at a judge in a short gown who would tremble before a mere deputy magistrate in full robes. We must comply with the forms.

THE COUNT: Let the public in.

USHER [*opening the door*]: Court!

[*Enter* ANTONIO, *servants, peasants. The* COUNT *sits in his great chair,* BRID'OISON *beside him, the Clerk on his stool behind his table – magistrates and lawyers on side-benches,* MARCELINE *with* BARTHOLO *at her side,* FIGARO *on the other bench. Peasants standing behind.*]

BRID'OISON: Doublemain, call the case list.

DOUBLEMAIN [*reading a document*]: The noble, the most noble, most infinitely noble Don Pedro George, Hidalgo, Baron de los Altos, Y Montes Fieros, Y otros Montes: against Alonzo Calderon, dramatist. It's a case of a play – stillborn, which each disavows and attributes to the other.

THE COUNT: Very sensible of both of them! Verdict – to ensure some degree of success should they collaborate in another work, let the Nobleman give his name, the writer his talent!

DOUBLEMAIN [*reading again*]: Andre Petruchio, labourer, against the Provincial Treasurer – a case of arbitrary enforcement. . . .

THE COUNT: It's outside my competence. I shall serve my vassals better by interceding for them with the Crown. Next.

[DOUBLEMAIN, *picks up a third document.* BARTHOLO *and* FIGARO *rise.*]

DOUBLEMAIN: Barbe – Agar – Raab – Madeleine – Nicole – Marceline de Verte-Allure, spinster

[MARCELINE *rises and curtseys.*]

against Figaro – baptismal name not given.

FIGARO: Anonymous.

BRID'OISON: A-a-anonymous. Which patron saint is that?

FIGARO: Mine.

DOUBLEMAIN: Against Anonymous Figaro. Description?

FIGARO: Gentleman.

THE COUNT: *You* a gentleman?

   [*The Clerk is writing it down.*]

FIGARO: Had Heaven so willed I should have been the son of a princely house.

THE COUNT [*to the Clerk*]: Get on with it.

USHER [*barks*]: Silence, Gentlemen!

DOUBLEMAIN [*reading again*]: In the matter of an objection lodged against the marriage of the said Figaro by the aforesaid Verte-Allure, Dr Bartholo representing the plaintiff and the aforesaid Figaro pleading on his own behalf, if the Court will so permit, contrary though it be to the use and custom of the bar –

FIGARO: Use, Master Doublemain, is often an abuse. A client with any knowledge at all understands his case better than a lawyer starting from scratch and bawling at the top of his voice knowing everything except his brief and equally unconcerned about ruining his client, putting the justices to sleep, and boring everybody in Court. Such fellows are more puffed up than if they had composed one of Cicero's Orations. For my own part I shall put the facts in a few words. . . . Gentlemen . . .

DOUBLEMAIN: This is all beside the point. You aren't the plaintiff. Your job is to defend yourself. Come forward, Doctor, and read the promise of marriage.

FIGARO: Ay, let's have the promise.

BARTHOLO [*putting on spectacles*]: It is in precise terms.

BRID'OISON: We must have it produced.

DOUBLEMAIN: Silence then, Gentlemen!

USHER [*barks*]: Silence!

BARTHOLO [*reads*]: I the undersigned acknowledge having received from the aforesaid Miss . . . etc. Marceline de Verte-Allure the sum of two thousand milled-edge piastres –

which sum I will repay on demand at the Castle and in consideration of which I will marry her – etc. etc. Signed Figaro – plain Figaro. The claim is for repayment of the money and execution of the undertaking with costs. A more interesting case, Gentlemen, was never submitted to the jurisdiction of the Court. Since the day when Alexander the Great made a promise of marriage to the fair Thalestris ...

THE COUNT: Before we proceed any further, is there agreement on the validity of the document?

BRID'OISON: Have you anything to say against the document as read?

FIGARO: I contend that there was malice, error, or deliberate misrepresentation in the reading of the document, the words, as written, being not 'which sum I will repay her *and* I will marry her' but 'which sum I will repay her *or* I will marry her'.

THE COUNT: Is the word in the document 'and' or 'or'?

BARTHOLO: It's 'and'.

FIGARO: 'Or'.

BRID'OISON: D-Doublemain, read it yourself.

DOUBLEMAIN: It's always safer: parties to the case often misrepresent in reading. [*Reads*] 'M, 'm, 'm, ... Miss 'm, 'm, 'm, Verte-Allure ... repay upon demand at the castle and ... or, and – or ... the word's badly written ... and there's a blot. ...

BRID'OISON: A b-b-blot? I know these blots.

BARTHOLO: My case is that it is the coordinating conjunction 'and' linking the coordinate clauses 'I will pay the lady' *and* 'I will marry her'.

FIGARO: And I maintain that it is the alternating conjunction *or* which separates the two clauses – I pay the damsel *or* I espouse her. As for this pedant, I'll out-pedant him; if he's for talking Latin I'll talk Greek and wipe the floor with him.

THE COUNT: How is one to decide such a question?

BARTHOLO: To cut the matter short, Gentlemen, and not to quibble about a single word – we'll concede that it was 'or'.

FIGARO: I want that recorded.

BARTHOLO: Agreed. The guilty won't escape by resorting to a miserable get-out like that. Let us examine the document in another sense – [*Reads*] 'Which sum I will repay to her at the Castle where I will marry her.' Just as one might say, Gentlemen, 'You'll be bled in this bed *where* you'll stay and keep warm.' That is to say '*in which*'. 'You shall take two grains of rhubarb wherein you shall mix a pinch of tamarind' – 'in which you shall mix'. So 'the Castle *where* I will marry her' – 'the Castle *in which* – *wherein* –'

FIGARO: Not a bit of it! The passage is intended to be read in this sense – 'Either the malady will kill you *or* the doctor will' – *or else* the doctor will, it's beyond question. Another example – 'Either you'll write nothing readable *or* fools will run down your work' – 'or fools' – The sense is clear, for in this case either fools or knaves, you may be sure, are the governing substantives. Does Master Bartholo think I have forgotten my grammar? 'I will repay her at the Castle – comma – *or* I will marry her.'*

BARTHOLO [*sharply*]: No comma.

FIGARO: Oh, yes, there *is* a comma, Gentlemen. 'Comma, or else I will marry her.'

BARTHOLO [*glancing quickly at the paper*]: No comma, Gentlemen.

FIGARO [*quickly*]: It *was* there, Gentlemen. Besides, if a man marries can he be held to repay his spouse?

BARTHOLO: Yes. We marry but keep separate properties.

---

* The play on the meaning of '*où*' = 'where' and '*ou*' = 'or' is untranslatable. In performance in English it is well to cut from Bartholo's speech 'To cut the matter short, Gentlemen' to the stage direction *The judges rise to discuss this in whispers* below.

FIGARO: *We* keep separate persons if marriage doesn't make us quits.

[*The judges rise to discuss this in whispers.*]

BARTHOLO: That's a fine way of acquitting yourself.

DOUBLEMAIN: Silence, Gentlemen!

USHER [*barks*]: Silence!

BARTHOLO: And the scoundrel calls that paying his debts!

FIGARO: Are you pleading your case, Sir, or aren't you?

BARTHOLO: I'm defending this lady.

FIGARO: Then keep on talking nonsense but cut out the insults. When the Courts, fearing that litigants might be carried away by their feelings, allowed so-called third parties to plead for them, they never intended that these disinterested advocates should come to enjoy the privilege of being impudent with impunity – it's degrading a noble institution.

[*The judges continue their discussion in whispers.*]

ANTONIO [*to Marceline, indicating the judges*]: What are they jabbering about?

MARCELINE: Someone has got at the presiding judge and now he's getting at the others – result – I'm losing my case.

BARTHOLO [*gloomily*]: I fear so.

FIGARO [*gaily*]: Courage, Marceline!

DOUBLEMAIN [*getting up and addressing Marceline*]: That's going too far! I denounce you! I demand in the interests of the honour of the Court that a judgement be given on this matter before proceeding to the other offences.

THE COUNT [*sitting down*]: No, my dear Clerk, I shall pass no opinion on the personal reflection. A Spanish judge need not blush for excesses more fitly attributable to Asiatic tribunals. There are sufficient other abuses! I mean to correct a second one by giving you the justification of my decision: any judge who declines to do so is an enemy of the laws. What can the plaintiff legitimately demand? Marriage in default of payment. The two together would be incompatible.

DOUBLEMAIN: Silence, Gentlemen.

USHER [*barks*]: Silence!

THE COUNT: What reply does the defendant make? If he wishes to retain his freedom he may do so.

FIGARO [*joyfully*]: I've won!

THE COUNT: But since the document says 'which sum I will pay immediately upon demand or I will marry,' etc., the Court condemns the defendant to pay two thousand piastres to the plaintiff or to marry her *today*. [*He rises.*]

FIGARO [*stupefied*]: I've lost!

ANTONIO [*joyfully*]: A splendid judgement!

FIGARO: What's splendid about it?

ANTONIO: Splendid that you aren't going to be my nephew. Thank you very much, My Lord!

USHER [*barks*]: Pass along, Gentlemen.

[*People go out.*]

ANTONIO: I must go tell my niece all this. [*Exit.*]

MARCELINE [*sitting down*]: Ah! I breathe again.

FIGARO: And I'm stifling!

THE COUNT [*aside*]: At least I have got my own back. That's some satisfaction!

FIGARO [*aside*]: And that fellow Bazile who was to have put in an objection to Marceline's marriage, where's he got to? [*To the Count, who is going out*] You are leaving us, My Lord?

THE COUNT: The judgement is given.

FIGARO [*to Brid'oison*]: It's this great windbag of a counsellor. . . .

BRID'OISON: A windbag, me?

FIGARO: Yes. And I shan't marry her. *I'll* play the gentleman for once. [*The Count stops.*]

BARTHOLO: You'll marry her.

FIGARO: Without the permission of my noble parents?

BARTHOLO: Where are they? Show us them.

FIGARO: Give me a little time. I'm pretty near to finding them. I've been seeking them fifteen years.

BARTHOLO: The foolish braggart! He's some foundling or other.

FIGARO: Not found but lost, Doctor, or possibly stolen.

THE COUNT: Lost or stolen, where's your proof? Or will he say that's an insult?

FIGARO: My Lord! If the lace shawls, embroidered wrappings, and jewels the brigands found on me did not indicate high birth, the precautions someone had taken to give me marks of distinction would be sufficient testimony that I was a child someone valued: this mysterious letter on my arm. [*Rolls up his sleeve.*]

MARCELINE [*jumping up quickly*]: A spatula on your right arm!

FIGARO: How do you know it?

MARCELINE: Heavens, 'tis he!

FIGARO: It's me all right!

BARTHOLO: And who is he?

MARCELINE: Emmanuel!

BARTHOLO: You were stolen by gipsies?

FIGARO [*excited*]: Near a castle. Good Doctor, if you restore me to my noble house put your own price upon the service: mountains of money wouldn't deter my illustrious parents.

BARTHOLO [*pointing to Marceline*]: Behold your mother!

FIGARO: Foster mother?

BARTHOLO: Your own mother!

THE COUNT: His *mother*!

FIGARO: Explain yourself.

MARCELINE [*pointing to Bartholo*]: Behold your father!

FIGARO [*desolated*]: Oh, oh, oh! Have pity on me!

MARCELINE: Has nature not told you so a thousand times?

FIGARO: Never!

THE COUNT [*aside*]: His *mother*!

BRID'OISON: He won't marry her. That's clear.

(BARTHOLO: Nor I either!*

MARCELINE: Nor you! And what about your son? Did you not swear to me ...

BARTHOLO: I was a fool. If such old associations were binding, there's no saying who one would have to marry.

BRID'OISON: And if we looked at it carefully enough, no one would marry anybody.

BARTHOLO: Faults so notorious. A deplorable youth –

MARCELINE [*warming to it by degrees*]: Ay! Deplorable! More so than you think! I won't attempt to deny my faults – they have been fully exposed today! But it's hard to have to expiate them after thirty years of decent living. I was by nature good and so remained as long as I was allowed to do so, but just at the age when we are beset by illusions, inexperience, and necessity, when seducers besiege us and want stabs us in the back, what can a young girl do against the serried ranks of her enemies? The very man who judges us so severely now has probably compassed the ruin of a dozen such unfortunates himself!

FIGARO: Those who are most blameworthy are the least generous themselves. That's always the way!

MARCELINE: You men, lost to all sense of obligation, who stigmatize with your contempt the playthings of your passions – your unfortunate victims! It's you who ought to be punished for the errors of our youth – you and your

---

* The passage in brackets was omitted in the original production at the instance of the actors but Beaumarchais restored the cuts in the printed version of the play.

magistrates so vain of their right to judge us, you who by your culpable negligence allow us to be deprived of all honest means of existence. What is there for these unhappy girls to do? They had a natural right to make all feminine apparel and yet they let thousands of men be trained to it.

FIGARO [*furiously*]: They even set soldiers to embroidery!

MARCELINE [*carried away by her own eloquence*]: Even in the more exalted walks of life you accord us women no more than a derisory consideration. In a state of servitude behind the alluring pretences of respect, treated as children where our possessions are concerned we are punished as responsible adults where our faults are in question! Ah! Whatever way one looks at it your conduct towards us must provoke horror or compassion!

FIGARO: She's right!

THE COUNT [*aside*]: All too much so.

BRID'OISON: My God! How right she is!

MARCELINE: But what if an unjust man denies us justice, my son? Think no more about whence you came but whither you are bound. That is all that matters to any of us. Within a few months your fiancée will be her own mistress: she'll accept you: that I'll answer for. Live, then, henceforward in company of a loving wife and mother who will be rivals only in affection for you. Be indulgent towards them and rejoice in your happiness, my son; be gay, free, open-hearted with all the world: your mother will seek no other happiness.

FIGARO: You speak wonderfully persuasively, Mother, but I hold to my own opinion. What fools we are indeed! Here the world's been turning for thousands and thousands of years, and in face of that ocean of time, from which I've chanced to snatch some miserable thirty years or so that will never come again, I'm tormenting myself over the question of whom I owe them to. So much the worse for those who bother about such things! Spending one's life on such trivial worries means pulling against the collar with never a break, like the miserable horses on the tow-paths of our rivers: even when they come to a halt they still keep on pulling. We'll take what comes to us.)

THE COUNT: This nonsensical business is spoiling my plans.

BRID'OISON [*to Figaro*]: And the noble birth and the castle you talked of? You were trying to impose upon justice.

FIGARO: And a fine trick Justice was going to make me do. After all the times I've refrained from breaking this gentleman's neck because of his cursed hundred crowns – he now turns out to be my father! However, since Heaven has prevented me from committing a crime, accept my apologies, Father. And you, Mother, embrace me – as maternally as you can.

[*As* MARCELINE *embraces him,* SUZANNE *runs in with a purse in her hand, followed by* ANTONIO.]

SUZANNE: Stop them, My Lord! Don't let them marry. My Mistress has given me the money to pay her!

THE COUNT: The Devil take her mistress! It seems they are all in conspiracy together! [*He goes out.*]

ANTONIO [*seeing* FIGARO *embracing his mother*]: Hey! Wait a bit, lass, before you start paying.

SUZANNE: I have seen enough: come along, Uncle.

FIGARO [*stopping her*]: No, you don't! What have you seen?

SUZANNE: My own folly and your baseness.

FIGARO: Neither the one nor the other.

SUZANNE [*angrily*]: You can jolly well marry her, since you show such affection for her.

FIGARO (*gaily*): Affectionate we are, but there's no question of marrying.

[SUZANNE *makes to go but* FIGARO *detains her.*]

SUZANNE [*giving him a slap*]: And you have the audacity to try to keep me here!

FIGARO [*to the company*]: I ask you! That's not very loving, is it? [*To Suzanne*] Before you leave us I ask you to take a look at this lady.

SUZANNE: I *am* looking at her.

FIGARO: And what do you think of her?

SUZANNE: She's horrible!

FIGARO: Jealousy! Jealousy! One can always rely on it!

MARCELINE: Come and embrace your mother-to-be, my dear Suzanne. This naughty man who is teasing you so is my very own son.

SUZANNE [*running to her*]: You are his mother?
    [*They embrace.*]

ANTONIO: Has it just happened?

FIGARO: So far as I know.

MARCELINE: No, my heart was drawn to him. Only in my motive was I mistaken. It was blood calling to blood.

FIGARO: In my case my own good sense served me for instinct when I refused you. It wasn't that I ever disliked you. After all, I borrowed your money.

MARCELINE: It's yours now. Take your agreement. It can be your wedding gift.

SUZANNE [*giving him the purse*]: And take this too.

FIGARO: Thank you very much.

MARCELINE: Unhappy as a girl, I was about to become the most miserable of wives, and here I am now the most fortunate of mothers: embrace me, my children. In you all my affections unite. My happiness is complete. Ah! My children, how I shall love you!

FIGARO [*touched himself*]: Go easy, mother! Would you have me drown my eyes with the first tears I have ever known? At any rate they are tears of joy. But how stupid of me. I was almost ashamed of them. I felt them trickling between my fingers and tried to restrain them: away with pride! I'll laugh and cry at the same time: one doesn't have such an experience twice. [*Embraces his mother and Suzanne – one on either side of him.*]

MARCELINE: Oh, my dear boy!

SUZANNE: Oh, my dear boy!

BRID'OISON [*wiping his eyes with his handkerchief*]: Ay well! Can it be that I'm getting silly too?

FIGARO [*exalted*]: Misfortune! Now I can defy you! Touch me now if you can with these two dear women to protect me!

ANTONIO [*to Figaro*]: Less of your blarney if you don't mind! When it comes to marrying into a family it's well that the parents should be married first. You understand? Have yours joined hands yet?

BARTHOLO: Have I given my hand? May it wither and drop off before I give it to the mother of such a fool.

ANTONIO: Then you are no father at all! [*To Figaro*] In that case, my lad, there's no more to be said.

SUZANNE: Oh, Uncle!

ANTONIO: Am I going to give my own sister's daughter to a fellow who's nobody's child?

BRID'OISON: How can that be, you fool? We are all somebody's children.

ANTONIO: Fiddle-de-dee! He shan't have her – never! [*Goes out.*]

BARTHOLO [*to Figaro*]: Go and find someone else to adopt you!

[*He is about to go, but* MARCELINE *throws her arms about him and brings him back.*]

MARCELINE: Stay, Doctor! Don't go!

FIGARO [*aside*]: Ay! It seems that all the fools in Andalusia are out to hinder my marriage.

SUZANNE [*to Bartholo*]: Dear father, he's your son!

MARCELINE [*to Bartholo*]: In ability, in brains, and in looks!

FIGARO [*to Bartholo*]: And he hasn't cost you a farthing.

BARTHOLO: What about the hundred crowns that he robbed me of?

MARCELINE [*stroking him*]: We shall take such care of you, papa!

SUZANNE [*likewise – other side*]: We shall all be so proud of you, daddy dear!

BARTHOLO [*weakening*]: Father, papa, daddy dear! It seems that I'm even sillier than this gentleman here [*indicating Brid'oison*]. I'm giving way like a child. [MARCELINE *and* SUZANNE *kiss him.*] No, no! I haven't said yes. [*Turning away*] What's happened to His Lordship?

FIGARO: Let's go to him and make him give the final word! If he's allowed to start any more trickery we shall be back where we started.

ALL: Come along. Hurry!

[*They drag Bartholo with them.*]

BRID'OISON [*alone*]: Sillier than this gentleman here! There are things one can say to oneself . . . they really are a rude lot round here!

ACT FOUR

SCENE: *A gallery with candelabra, hung with flowers and garlands all ready for a fête. Downstage left a writing-table with an armchair behind it.*

FIGARO [*his arm about Suzanne*]: Well, my love, are you content? This silver-tongued mother of mine has converted her Doctor. Little as he likes it, he's going to marry her and your scoundrelly uncle will be silenced: the only one who's still annoyed is His Lordship, for our marriage now becomes the price of theirs. Do laugh at this happy ending!

SUZANNE: Was anything ever so strange?

FIGARO: Or so amusing! We only planned to extract a dowry from His Excellency: we already have two which owe nothing to him. You had a desperate rival; I was tormented by a fury; instead we now have the kindest of mothers. Yesterday I was – as it were – alone in the world; now I have both my parents – not so grand, it's true, as I had imagined them but good enough for us – who lack the vanity of the wealthy.

SUZANNE: All the same, my boy, not one of the things you had planned, and we were expecting, has come true.

FIGARO: Chance has done better than any of us could, my dear. That's the way things are: one works, one schemes, one arranges things in one way: fortune determines them otherwise: from the insatiable conqueror who would gobble up the whole earth to the poor harmless blind creature who lets himself be led by his dog, we are all at the mercy of fortune's caprices: what's more, the blind man with his dog is often better guided, less deceived in his purposes than the other blind man with his train of dependants.

As for the blind god whom we call Love ... [*He takes her tenderly in his arms.*]

SUZANNE: He's the only one who interests me!

FIGARO: Allow me then – to pursue the foolish metaphor – to be your faithful dog that brings love to your pretty little door – and there we are installed for life!

SUZANNE: Love and you?

FIGARO: Me and love.

SUZANNE: And you'll not seek any other abode?

FIGARO: If you ever catch me I'm willing that a thousand million lovers ...

SUZANNE: You are beginning to exaggerate! Stick to the truth.

FIGARO: My truth is *the* truth.

SUZANNE: Fie! You rascal! Is there more than one sort?

FIGARO: Why yes! Of course! Ever since someone first noticed that in the course of time old follies become wisdom and little seeds of falsehood blossom from modest beginnings into great truths there have been a thousand varieties. There are the truths one knows but dare not divulge – for not all truths can be spoken; those one subscribes to without really believing – for not all truths are acceptable; lovers' vows, mothers' threats, statements made in drink, promises of men in high position, the final word of our merchants – there's no end to them. There's only one truth worth relying on – that's my love for Suzie.

SUZANNE: I love to hear you talk nonsense. It shows how happy you are. But now let's talk about my rendezvous with the Count.

FIGARO: Or rather let's never mention it! It nearly cost me my Suzanne.

SUZANNE: Don't you want it to take place then?

FIGARO: If you love me, Suzie – promise me faithfully to let him go and shiver there alone and serve him right!

SUZANNE: It was much more difficult to say yes to him than it will be to say no. That's decided then.

FIGARO: The truth – you really mean that?

SUZANNE: I'm not like you clever ones – I only know one sort of truth.

FIGARO: And you'll love me a little?

SUZANNE: Lots and lots!

FIGARO: That's not much!

SUZANNE: What d'you mean?

FIGARO: When it comes to love, you know, even too much isn't enough.

SUZANNE: I don't follow these subtleties, but I shall love none but my husband.

FIGARO: Stick to that and you'll be a wonderful exception to the rule. [*He endeavours to kiss her as the* COUNTESS *enters.*]

THE COUNTESS: Ah! I was quite right! Wherever they are, I said, they'll be together. Come, Figaro, it's anticipating the future to be having your *tête-à-tête* now. Your master is wanting you.

FIGARO: True, Madam, I'm forgetting myself. I'll take my excuse with me. [*Endeavours to take Suzanne.*]

THE COUNTESS [*detaining her*]: She shall follow you. [*To Suzanne*] Have you arranged for our change of clothes?

SUZANNE: It won't be needed. The rendezvous is off.

THE COUNTESS: Ah! So you have changed your mind?

SUZANNE: It's Figaro.

THE COUNTESS: You are deceiving me.

SUZANNE: Heavens, no!

THE COUNTESS: Figaro isn't the man to let a dowry slip

SUZANNE: Ah, Madam, what do you mean?

THE COUNTESS: You have come to an understanding with the Count, so you now regret that you told me his plans. I can see through you. Leave me. [*She makes to go out.*]

SUZANNE [*kneeling before her*]: In Heaven's name and as I hope for salvation, you don't know, Madam, how much you wrong me. After all your goodness and the dowry you have given me . . .

THE COUNTESS [*raising her*]: Alas . . . I don't know what I'm saying! Let me take your place in the garden – so, you'll avoid going yourself, keep faith with your husband, and help me to bring mine back to me.

SUZANNE: But how you have hurt me!

THE COUNTESS: I was just being stupid! [*She kisses her forehead.*] Where is your rendezvous?

SUZANNE: The garden is all I remember.

THE COUNTESS [*pointing to the table*]: Take this pen and let us arrange a place.

SUZANNE: Write to *him*?

THE COUNTESS: You must.

SUZANNE: But Your Ladyship, surely it's you who should . . .

THE COUNTESS: I'll take the responsibility.

[SUZANNE *sits down and the* COUNTESS *dictates.*]

The latest song – the tune 'May it be fine tonight beneath the chestnut trees – may it be fine – tonight'.

SUZANNE [*writing*]: '. . . beneath the chestnut trees', and then?

THE COUNTESS: Do you think he'll not understand?

SUZANNE [*reading it again*]: It's all right. [*Folds the note.*] How are we to seal it?

THE COUNTESS: Pin it. Quick! It will serve for the reply. Write on the outside, 'Send back the seal.'

SUZANNE [*writes laughing*]: Ah! The seal. This is even more amusing than . . . the affair of the warrant.

THE COUNTESS [*sadly*]: Ah!

SUZANNE [*searching*]: I haven't a pin.

THE COUNTESS [*opening her dress*]: Take this one. [*The ribbon falls to the ground.*] Ah, my ribbon!

SUZANNE [*picking it up*]: It's that little robber's. How could you be so cruel!

THE COUNTESS: Could I let him keep it on his arm? That would have been a nice thing. Give it to me!

SUZANNE: Your Ladyship isn't going to keep it – all stained with that young man's blood?

THE COUNTESS: It will do for Fanchette. The first time she brings me a nosegay . . .

[*Enter* CHÉRUBIN *dressed as a shepherdess*, FANCHETTE *and other girls carrying bouquets.*]

FANCHETTE: Your Ladyship. Here are the village girls bringing flowers for you.

THE COUNTESS [*quickly putting away the ribbon*]: Charming! I'm sorry that I don't know you all. [*Points to Chérubin.*] Who is this charming child who has so modest an air?

A SHEPHERDESS: She's a cousin of mine, Madam. Just here for the wedding.

THE COUNTESS: She's charming. Since I can't hold twenty bouquets we'll do honour to the stranger. [*Takes Chérubin's bouquet and kisses 'her' forehead.*] She's blushing! [*To Suzanne*] Suzanne, don't you think she's like someone . . .

SUZANNE: Yes – almost to the life!

CHÉRUBIN [*aside, hands on his heart*]: Ah! How I've longed for that kiss!

[*Enter the* COUNT *and* ANTONIO.]

ANTONIO: I tell you he's here, My Lord: they changed his clothes in my daughter's room – all his own things are there still and here's his soldier's cap – I picked it up.

[*He goes up to the girls – looks along the line, recognizes Chérubin, and plucks off his woman's bonnet so that his hair falls down straight to his shoulders. He puts the military cap on Chérubin's head.*]

Ay! By Gad! There's our officer!

THE COUNTESS [*recoils*]: Heavens!

SUZANNE: The scamp!

ANTONIO: Didn't I say he was here!

THE COUNT [*angrily*]: Well, Madam!

THE COUNTESS: Well, Sir! I'm more surprised than you are – and no less annoyed.

THE COUNT: Yes, but what do you say now about what happened this morning?

THE COUNTESS: I mustn't keep up the deception any further. He had come down to my room – we started the joke which these young people here have continued. You took us by surprise while we were dressing him. Your first reaction was so violent that he took to flight: I was upset – and the fright we were all in did the rest.

THE COUNT [*angrily to Chérubin*]: Why didn't you go?

CHÉRUBIN [*snatching off his cap*]: My Lord, I . . .

THE COUNT: I shall punish your disobedience.

FANCHETTE [*thoughtlessly*]: Oh, Your Lordship! Listen to me! Whenever you come wanting to kiss me, you always say, 'I'll give you anything you like if only you'll love me, my little Fanchette!'

THE COUNT [*blushing*]: *I* say that?

FANCHETTE: Yes, Your Lordship! So instead of punishing Chérubin let me marry him and I'll love you to distraction.

THE COUNT [*aside*]: To be bewitched by a page!

THE COUNTESS: Well, Sir, it's your turn now. This child's confession, as naïve as my own, confirms a double truth. Any cause for disquiet I may give you is always unintentional, but you do everything possible to justify mine.

ANTONIO: You as well, My Lord! Egad! I shall have to straighten her up as I did her mother. . . . It's not that it matters now, but as Her Ladyship knows very well, little girls when they grow up . . .

THE COUNT [*aside, disconcerted*]: Some evil genius here turns everything to my disadvantage.

[*Enter* FIGARO.]

FIGARO: My Lord, if you are going to detain our young ladies we shan't be able to start either the fête or the dancing.

THE COUNT: Dancing? *You* dance? What are you thinking about? After falling this morning and spraining your ankle!

FIGARO [*shaking his foot*]: I still feel it a little, but it's nothing. [*To the girls*] Come along, my beauties. Come along.

THE COUNT [*detaining him*]: You were lucky that the flower-beds were so soft to fall on.

FIGARO: Very lucky! Otherwise ...

ANTONIO [*detaining him*]: But then he curled himself up as he jumped!

FIGARO: I suppose a better jumper would have remained in mid-air, eh? Come along, ladies!

ANTONIO [*detaining him*]: And all the time the page was on his horse and galloping towards Seville, eh?

FIGARO: Galloping or cantering ...

THE COUNT: And you with his warrant in your pocket.

FIGARO [*a little surprised*]: Of course! Why all this questioning? Come along, girls.

ANTONIO [*catching Chérubin by the waist*]: There's one here can prove my future nephew a liar.

FIGARO: Chérubin! [*Aside*] Confound the little fool!

ANTONIO: You get it now, eh?

FIGARO [*thinking rapidly*]: Yes, I get it. I get it. What tale is *he* telling?

THE COUNT: His tale is that he did the jumping into the wall-flowers.

FIGARO: Well – it could be – if he says so. I don't dispute what I know nothing about.

THE COUNT: So you and he both ...

FIGARO: Why not? Jumping can be infectious. Remember

Panurge's sheep. And when Your Lordship is in a temper most people would prefer to risk ¦ . . .

THE COUNT: What, two at a time?

FIGARO: Two dozen at a time. But what does it matter since no one was hurt? [*To the girls*] Are you coming or not?

THE COUNT [*annoyed*]: Is this a play we are acting?
[*Fanfare off.*]

FIGARO: That's the signal for the procession. To your positions ladies! Come, Suzanne, give me your arm.

[*All run off, leaving Chérubin behind. He hangs his head.*]

THE COUNT [*watching Figaro go*]: The audacity! As for you, Master Sly-boots – who pretend to be ashamed of yourself now – go and get dressed at once and don't let me set eyes on you at tonight's entertainment.

THE COUNTESS: He's going to be terribly bored.

CHÉRUBIN [*thoughtlessly*]: Bored? A certain imprint on my forehead would compensate for a hundred years' confinement. [*Puts his cap on and runs off.*]

THE COUNT: What imprint has he on his forehead that he's so pleased about?

THE COUNTESS [*embarrassed*]: Of his – first soldier's cap. Everything's a toy for children his age. [*She is going out.*]

THE COUNT: Are you not staying?

THE COUNTESS: You know I'm not feeling well.

THE COUNT: Stay awhile for the sake of your protégée, or I shall believe you are annoyed.

THE COUNTESS: Here come the wedding parties. Let us sit and receive them.

THE COUNT: Weddings! I suppose one must put up with what one cannot prevent.

[*They sit down at one side of the stage. Enter the bridal parties to the tune of Les Folies d'Espagne. First huntsmen with shouldered guns. The alguazil, the magistrate, and* BRID'OI-SON, *peasants in holiday costume, girls carrying the bridal*]

crown, some with the veil, some with gloves and bouquet. AN-
TONIO *gives his hand to Suzanne as the one who is to give her
away: other young girls carry another set of bridal regalia for
Marceline.* FIGARO *gives his hand to Marceline, he being the
one who will give her away (to the* DOCTOR, *who brings up the
rear with a great bouquet). The peasants, having taken up
positions on opposite sides of the stage, dance the fandango.
While the refrain is being played* ANTONIO *brings Suzanne
forward to the Count and she kneels before him. While the*
COUNT *presents her with the bridal toque, the veil, and the
bouquet, two girls sing:*

> Young wife about to be sing the glory and the praise
> Of a Lord who is renouncing a right of former days!
> Forgoing his own pleasure your honour he prefers
> And on a happy husband a virgin bride confers!

SUZANNE *is kneeling, and during the last words of the verse she
pulls at the Count's coat and shows him the note which she is
holding: then she brings the hand nearest the audience in which
she holds the letter up to her head and as the* COUNT *makes us
if to adjust her toque she gives it to him. He puts it inside his
breast pocket; the singing finishes;* SUZANNE *rises and makes
a deep curtsey.* FIGARO *receives her from the Count and returns with her to the opposite side of the stage near to Marceline
while the fandango is danced again. The* COUNT *seeks an opportunity to read the letter and withdraws towards the wings, but
as he draws it from his coat he makes the gesture of a man
pricked by a pin. He shakes his finger, presses it, sucks it, and
looks at the paper.*]

THE COUNT: Confound the way women stick pins everywhere.

FIGARO [*who has seen everything, to his mother and Suzanne*]: It's
a love-letter from some young woman. The pin has had the
audacity to prick him.

[*During the foregoing speeches the orchestra plays* pianissimo.

The dance is resumed. The COUNT *has read the letter, turned it over, and seen the invitation to return the pin. He looks for it on the ground, picks it up, and sticks it in his sleeve.*]

FIGARO: Everything is precious that belongs to the loved one. See how he picks up the pin! Ah, what a fellow he is!

[*Meanwhile* SUZANNE *exchanges signs with the* COUNTESS, *the dance finishes, and the chorus begins again.* FIGARO *brings up Marceline and the* COUNT *is about to take the crown when there is an interruption.*]

USHER [*at the door*]: Stop, gentlemen! You can't all come in! Help me, guards!

[*Guards move to the door.*]

THE COUNT: What is it?

USHER: My Lord, it's Don Bazile. The whole village is following him. He's still singing as he goes.

THE COUNT: Let him come in, alone!

THE COUNTESS: Permit me to retire.

THE COUNT: I appreciate your forbearance.

THE COUNTESS: Suzanne! She'll come back. [*Aside to Suzanne*] Come along and let us change clothes.

[*They go out together.*]

MARCELINE: He always comes at the wrong time.

FIGARO: I'll make him sing small.

[*Enter* BAZILE *with his guitar and* GRIPE-SOLEIL.]

BAZILE [*singing*]:

> Let those whose love is firm and true
> Despise the love that's fleeting.
> What harm if I should cast an eye
> On every girl I'm meeting?
> If love is not to fly away
> Then what has Cupid wings for, pray?
> If love is not to fly away
> Then what has Cupid wings for, pray?

FIGARO [*advancing to meet him*]: Ay! We all know what his

wings are for! But tell me, friend, what's all this noise about?

BAZILE [*pointing to Gripe-Soleil*]: So that, having proved my loyalty to His Lordship by diverting this gentleman who is His Lordship's guest, I may in my turn demand justice of him.

GRIPE-SOLEIL: Bah! My Lord! He ain't diverted me in the least. All them old fag-ends of tunes . . .

THE COUNT: Well, then, what do you want of me, Bazile?

BAZILE: What belongs to me. The hand of Marceline – and I'm here to oppose . . .

FIGARO: How long is it since you looked a fool in the face, Sir?

BAZILE: I am doing now.

FIGARO: Since my eyes make so good a mirror, take good note of my prediction. If you so much as show the slightest sign of coming near the lady . . .

BARTHOLO [*laughing*]: Why not? Let's hear what he has to say.

BRID'OISON [*coming between them*]: Why should two friends . . .

FIGARO: Friends! Us!

BAZILE: What an idea!

FIGARO: Just because he writes stupid music for church?

BAZILE: Because he scribbles his piffling verses?

FIGARO: A taproom warbler!

BAZILE: A newspaper hack!

FIGARO: An oratorio blockhead!

BAZILE: A diplomat jockey!

THE COUNT [*seated*]: They are equally insolent.

BAZILE: He never shows me any respect.

FIGARO: True! But how could I?

BAZILE: Goes about calling me a fool everywhere.

FIGARO: So you think I'm an echo?

BAZILE: Whereas there's never a singer I don't set on the road to success.

FIGARO: Set off bawling, you mean!

BAZILE: There he goes again!

FIGARO: And why not, if it's the truth? Are you a prince of the blood that one has to flatter you? Since there's nothing to be got from lying to you, you must put up with the truth, you idiot. Anyhow, if you are frightened of our telling you the truth, why do you come interfering with our marriage?

BAZILE [*to Marceline*]: Did you – or did you not – promise me that if you weren't fixed up within four years you'd give me the chance?

MARCELINE: On what condition did I promise it?

BAZILE: That if you could find a certain lost child I should adopt him.

ALL: He's found!

BAZILE: He can't be!

ALL [*indicating Figaro*]: Here he is!

BAZILE [*recoiling*]: The Devil!

BRID'OISON: So ... you renounce your claim to the mother?

BAZILE: Could anything be worse than to be thought the father of a scoundrel?

FIGARO: To be thought the son! Are you getting at me?

BAZILE [*pointing to Figaro*]: Since this gentleman is apparently somebody here, then let me be a nobody. [*He goes out.*]

BARTHOLO [*laughing*]: Ha ha ha!

FIGARO [*jumping with joy*]: So I'm to have my wife in the end!

THE COUNT [*aside*]: And I my mistress!

BRID'OISON [*to Marceline*]: So everybody's satisfied.

THE COUNT: Let the two contracts be prepared. I will sign them.

ALL: *Vivat!* [*They go out.*]

THE COUNT: I too need to retire a while. [*Makes as if to go.*]

GRIPE-SOLEIL: And I mun see to fixing the fireworks under the big chestnut trees as instructed.

THE COUNT [*turning back*]: What fool has given such an instruction?

FIGARO: Why not?

THE COUNT [*sharply*]: The Countess is unwell! How is she going to see the display? It must be on the terrace in front of her apartments.

FIGARO: You hear, Gripe-Soleil? The terrace.

THE COUNT: Under the chestnuts! A fine idea! [*Aside as he goes*] They were going to light up my rendezvous! [*He goes.*]

FIGARO: He shows unusual consideration for his wife!

MARCELINE: A word with you, son. I want to make things straight with you. Mistaken impressions led me to do your wife an injustice: I thought she had an understanding with the Count, though Bazile always maintained that she kept him at a distance.

FIGARO: You don't understand your son if you think he can be upset by any aberrations of the female sex. I defy the cleverest of them to make a fool of me.

MARCELINE: There's no harm in thinking that, my son: jealousy . . .

FIGARO: Springs either from pride or from folly! I'm philosophic on that score – imperturbable! Should Suzanne ever deceive me, I pardon her beforehand. She'll have her work cut out!

[*Enter* FANCHETTE.]

Ah, my little cousin is eavesdropping!

FANCHETTE: No. No, I'm not – they say it's naughty to listen.

FIGARO: True, but it's useful: people don't always realize that.

FANCHETTE: I was looking to see if there was anyone here.

FIGARO: One fib already, you scamp! You know that he couldn't be . . .

FANCHETTE: Who?

FIGARO: Chérubin.

FANCHETTE: I'm not looking for him. I know where he is. It's my cousin, Suzanne.

FIGARO: And what does my little cousin want with her?

FANCHETTE: I'll tell you since you are my cousin now – it's only a pin I have to give back to her.

FIGARO: A pin! A pin! From whom, you minx? So young and already plying your trade. . . . [*Recovers his self-control.*] You have done very well, Fanchette. It's very kind of my little cousin. . . .

FANCHETTE: Then what are you so annoyed about? I'm going.

FIGARO [*detaining her*]: No, no! I'm only joking; look, your little pin is the one His Lordship told you to give back to Suzanne: it was used to fasten up a note that he held in his hand. You see I know all about it.

FANCHETTE: Then if you know all this why do you ask about it?

FIGARO [*fishing*]: Because it would be amusing to know how His Lordship contrived to give you the pin.

FANCHETTE [*naïvely*]: Just as you said. 'Here, little Fanchette, give this pin to your fair cousin and just say that it's the seal for the big chestnut trees.'

FIGARO: The big –?

FANCHETTE: Chestnut trees. It's true that he added, 'Take care nobody sees you.'

FIGARO: And you must do as you were told, cousin. Fortunately nobody has seen you. So go do your job nicely and don't tell Suzanne anything but what His Lordship told you to do.

FANCHETTE: Why should I? He seems to take me for a fool, this new cousin of mine! [*Exit skipping.*]

FIGARO: Well, mother?

MARCELINE: Well, son?

FIGARO [*as if choking*]: Well it just shows – some things really are . . .

MARCELINE: What things?

FIGARO [*holding his chest*]: Something I've heard. It weighs as heavy as lead on my heart.

MARCELINE [*laughing*]: So all this assurance was nothing but an inflated balloon – one little pin deflates it.

FIGARO [*furious*]: But the pin was the one he picked up, mother!

MARCELINE [*recalling his words*]: Jealousy! Oh, 'I'm philosophic on that score! Should Suzanne ever deceive me I pardon her. . . .'

FIGARO: Oh mother! We talk as our feelings dictate. Put the coolest of judges to plead his own cause and see him expound the law! I see now why he was concerned about the fireworks! But as for the young lady with the pin, she isn't going to get away with it – she and her chestnuts! If I'm sufficiently married to give me the right to be angry – on the other hand, I'm not so much committed that I can't marry someone else and leave her to . . .

MARCELINE: A fine conclusion, I must say! Let's destroy ourselves on the merest suspicion! What proof have you, my boy, that she's deceiving you and not the Count? Have you some new insight into her character that you condemn her unheard? Are you sure that she'll go to the rendezvous? And why? Or what she'll say when she gets there? Or what she'll do when she does? I thought you had more sense!

FIGARO [*kissing her hand*]: My mother's right! She's right, right, always right! But let's allow something, mother, for human nature: we feel better for it afterwards. We'll look into it before accusing and taking action – I know the rendezvous. Good-bye, mother. [*Goes out.*]

MARCELINE: Good-bye. And I know as well. Having dealt with him, we'll see what Suzanne's up to, or rather we'll giver her a warning: she's such a pretty creature. Ah! How we poor downtrodden women are drawn to run to each other's help against these proud and terrible simpletons – men – when personal interest doesn't set us against each other!

ACT FIVE

SCENE: *A chestnut grove in a park; pavilions, kiosks, or garden temples are on either side; upstage is a clearing between two hedges; a garden seat downstage. It is dark.*

[FANCHETTE *alone, holding in one hand two biscuits and an orange, in the other a paper lantern, lighted.*]

FANCHETTE: In the left-hand pavilion, he said. That's this one. Supposing he were not here yet my little partner – those horrid people in the kitchen didn't even want to give me an orange and a couple of biscuits. . . . 'Who wants them?' 'Oh, well, Sir, they're for someone. . . .' 'Ah, we know!' Well, what if they do know! Just because His Lordship can't bear the sight of him, does he have to perish of hunger? Even then it cost me a kiss! Who knows, perhaps he'll repay me!

[*She sees* FIGARO, *who comes and looks closely at her. She cries out: 'Ah!,' then takes to her heels and runs across to the pavilion on her left.*]

FIGARO [*wearing a cloak and a hat with the wide brim turned down*]: It's Fanchette.

[*Enter* BARTHOLO, BAZILE, ANTONIO, BRID'OISON, GRIPE-SOLEIL, *valets, and workmen.*]

FIGARO [*fiercely, looking closely at each of the others as they arrive*]: Good evening, Gentlemen, good evening! Are you all here?

BAZILE: All whom you required to come.

FIGARO: About what time is it?

ANTONIO [*looking up*]: Moon should be up by now.

BARTHOLO: And what dark deeds are you up to now? He has a conspiratorial air!

197

FIGARO: I ask you! Didn't you come to the castle for a wedding?

BRID'OISON: Certainly.

ANTONIO: We were going down to the park to await the signal for the fête.

FIGARO: You won't need to go any farther, Gentlemen. It's here under the chestnuts that we are going to sing the praises of my worthy fiancée and the noble lord who has his own intentions in regard to her.

BAZILE [*recalling the day's events*]: Ah, yes, I know what it is! Take my advice and let's retire. It's a question of a rendez-vous. I'll tell you all about it later.

BRID'OISON [*to Figaro*]: We – we'll c-come back!

FIGARO: Don't fail to come at once when I call. You can blame me if you don't see something interesting.

BARTHOLO: Remember that a wise man doesn't meddle with the affairs of the great.

FIGARO: I'll remember.

BARTHOLO: They are always one up on us because of their rank.

FIGARO: Apart from their ingenious little ways which you are forgetting about. But remember also that once a man is known to be faint-hearted he's at the mercy of every rascal that comes along.

BARTHOLO: Very true.

FIGARO: And that I bear on my mother's side the honoured name of Verte-Allure.

BARTHOLO: The Devil's in him!

BRID'OISON: He is, he – is, he is!

BAZILE [*aside*]: The Count and Suzanne have managed without me! So I don't mind what trick he plays.

FIGARO [*to the servants*]: As for you others, knaves that you are, do as I told you and get the whole area lighted up or, by that death I wish I was at grips with, if I get hold of any of you – [*Seizes Gripe-Soleil by the arm.*]

GRIPE-SOLEIL [*goes off howling*]: Ah, oh, ooh! You brute!

BAZILE [*going*]: Heaven send you joy, Mr Bridegroom!
  [*They all go out.*]

FIGARO [*gloomily walking up and down in the dark*]: Oh, woman, woman, woman, feeble creature that you are! No living thing can fail to be true to its nature. Is it yours to deceive? After stubbornly refusing when I urged her to it in the presence of her mistress – at the very moment of her plighting her word to me, in the very midst of the ceremony . . . and he smiled while he read it, the scoundrel! And I standing by like a blockhead! No, My Lord Count, you shan't have her, you shall not have her! Because you are a great nobleman you think you are a great genius. . . . Nobility, fortune, rank, position! How proud they make a man feel! What have *you* done to deserve such advantages? Put yourself to the trouble of being born – nothing more! For the rest – a very ordinary man! Whereas I, lost among the obscure crowd, have had to deploy more knowledge, more calculation and skill merely to survive than has sufficed to rule all the provinces of Spain for a century! Yet you would measure yourself against me. . . . Somebody's coming – it's she! No, it's nobody at all. The night's as dark as the very devil and here am I plying the stupid trade of husband though I'm still only half married. [*Sits down.*] Could anything be stranger than a fate like mine? Son of goodness knows whom, stolen by bandits, brought up to their way of life, I become disgusted with it and yearn for an honest profession – only to find myself repulsed everywhere. I study Chemistry, Pharmacy, Surgery, and all the prestige of a great nobleman can barely secure me the handling of a horse-doctor's probe! Weary of making sick animals worse and determined to do something different, I throw myself headlong into the theatre. Alas, I might as well have put a stone round my neck! I fudge up a play about the manners of the Seraglio: a Spanish author, I imagined, could attack Mahomet without scruple, but, immediately, some envoy from goodness-knows-where complains that some of my lines offend the Sublime Porte, Persia, some part or other of the East Indies, the whole of Egypt, and the Kingdoms of Cyrenaica, Tripoli, Tunis, Algiers, and Morocco. Behold my play scuppered to please a set of Mohammedan princes – not one of whom I believe can read – who habitually beat a tattoo on our shoulders to the tune of 'Down with the Christian dogs!' Unable to break my spirit they decided to take it out of my body. My cheeks grew furrowed: my time was out. I saw in the distance the approach of the fell sergeant, his quill stuck into his wig: trembling I summoned all my resources. Economic matters were under discussion. Since one can talk about things even though one doesn't possess them – and though in fact I hadn't a penny, I wrote a treatise on the Theory of Value and its relation to the net product of national wealth. Whereupon I found myself looking from the depths of a hired carriage at the drawbridge of a castle, lowered for my reception, and abandoned all hope of liberty. [*Rises.*] How I would like to have hold of one of those Jacks in office – so indifferent to the evils that they cause – when disaster had extinguished his pride! I'd tell him that stupidities that appear in print acquire importance only in so far as their circulation is restricted, that unless there is liberty to criticize, praise has no value, and that only trivial minds are apprehensive of trivial scribbling. [*He sits again.*] Tiring of housing an obscure pensioner, they put me into the street eventually, and, since a man must eat even though he isn't in jail, I sharpen my quill again, inquire how things are going, and am told that during my economic retreat there had been established in

Madrid a system of free sale of commodities which extended even to the products of the press, and that, provided I made no reference in my articles to the authorities or to religion, or to politics, or to morals, or to high officials, or to influential organizations, or the Opera, or to any theatrical productions, or to anybody of any standing whatsoever, I could freely print anything I liked – subject to the approval of two or three censors! In order to profit from this very acceptable freedom I announce a new periodical which, not wishing to tread on anyone else's toes, I call the *Good for Nothing Journal*. Phew! A thousand miserable scribblers are immediately up in arms against me: my paper is suppressed and there I am out of work once again! I was on the point of giving up in despair when it occurred to someone to offer me a job. Unfortunately I had some qualification for it – it needed a knowledge of figures – but it was a dancer who got it! Nothing was left to me but stealing, so I set up as a banker at Faro. Now notice what happens! I dine out in style, and so-called fashionable people throw open their houses to me – keeping three-quarters of the profits for themselves. I could well have restored my fortunes! I even began to understand that in making money *savoir-faire* is more important than true knowledge. But since everybody was involved in some form of swindle and at the same time demanding honesty from me, I inevitably went under again. This time I renounced the world, and twenty fathoms of water might have divided me from it when a beneficent Providence recalled me to my original estate. I picked up my bundle and my leather strop and, leaving illusions to the fools who can live by them and my pride in the middle of the road as too heavy a burden for a pedestrian, I set out with my razor from town to town, and lived henceforward carefree. A great nobleman comes to Seville and he recognizes me. I get him safely married, and as a reward for my trouble in helping him to a wife he now wants to intercept mine! Intrigue! Plots – stormy interludes! I'm on the point of falling into an abyss and marrying my own mother when, lo and behold, my parents turn up one after the other! [*He rises.*] Debate and discussion. It's you, it's him, it's me, it's thee, no, it isn't any of us, no, who is it then? [*Falls into his seat again.*] Oh! Fantastic series of events! Why should they happen to me? Why these things and not others? Who made me responsible? Obliged to follow a road I set out on, all unknowing, and one I shall come to the end of, willy nilly, I have strewn it with such flowers as my high spirits have permitted: I say my high spirits without knowing whether they are any more mine than the rest or who is this 'me' that I'm worrying about: a formless aggregation of unidentified parts, then a puny stupid being, a frisky little animal, a young man ardent in the pursuits of pleasure with every taste for enjoyment, plying all sorts of trades in order to live – now master, now servant, as fortune pleases, ambitious from vanity, industrious from necessity, but lazy from inclination! Orator in emergency, poet for relaxation, musician when occasion demands, in love by mad fits and starts. I've seen everything, done everything, been everything. At last all illusions destroyed – disabused – all too much disabused – Oh, Suzie, Suzie, Suzie, what torture you put upon me! I hear someone coming. This is the moment of decision!

[*Withdraws off-stage – right. Enter the* COUNTESS, *dressed as Suzanne,* SUZANNE, *dressed as the Countess, and* MARCELINE.]

SUZANNE [*to the Countess in a whisper*]: Yes, Marceline told me that Figaro would be here.

MARCELINE: So he is. Lower your voice.

SUZANNE: So – one listens and the other comes looking for me. Let us begin.

MARCELINE: I don't mean to lose a word. I'll hide in this pavilion. [*Goes in where Fanchette is.*]

SUZANNE: Your Ladyship is trembling. Are you cold?

THE COUNTESS: The evening is damp. I'm going to go inside.

SUZANNE: If Your Ladyship doesn't need me I'll take the air a little under the trees.

THE COUNTESS: You'll get the dew on you.

SUZANNE: I'm prepared for it.

FIGARO [*aside*]: Oh, yes! For the dew!

    [SUZANNE *retires towards the alley opposite where Figaro is. Enter* CHÉRUBIN *in uniform singing gaily the chorus of his ballad.*]

CHÉRUBIN:

        Alas! My heart is in pain
        I shall ne'er see my true love again. . . .

THE COUNTESS [*aside*]: The page!

CHÉRUBIN [*stops*]: There's someone about! Let me get to my hiding-place where little Fanchette . . . It's a woman!

THE COUNTESS [*overhearing*]: Heavens!

CHÉRUBIN [*bending down and peering through the darkness*]: Am I mistaken? From the headdress and features I can just make out in the dark it seems to be Suzie.

THE COUNTESS [*aside*]: Supposing the Count were to come. . . .

    [*The* COUNT *appears upstage.*]

CHÉRUBIN [*approaching and taking the Countess's hand in spite of her attempts to avoid him*]: Yes, it's no other than our charming Suzie. Could I mistake this soft little hand and the way that it trembles – or the beating of my own heart?

    [*The* COUNTESS *draws her hand away.*]

THE COUNTESS [*in a whisper*]: Go away!

CHÉRUBIN: If it is pity that has drawn you to the part of of the park where I'm hiding . . .

THE COUNTESS: Figaro is coming.

THE COUNT [*coming downstage – aside*]: Isn't it Suzanne I see?

CHÉRUBIN: I'm not frightened of Figaro. It isn't him you are waiting for.

THE COUNTESS: Who is it, then?

THE COUNT [*aside*]: There's someone with her.

CHÉRUBIN: It's His Lordship, you hussy! He asked for a rendezvous with you when I was behind the chair this morning.

THE COUNT [*aside, furious*]: It's that infernal page again.

FIGARO [*aside*]: And they say one shouldn't eavesdrop!

SUZANNE [*aside*]: The little chatterer.

THE COUNTESS [*to the page*]: Be good enough to go away.

CHÉRUBIN: Not until I've received the reward of obedience.

THE COUNTESS [*alarmed*]: You have the audacity . . .

CHÉRUBIN [*with enthusiasm*]: Twenty kisses for yourself and then a hundred for your fair Mistress.

THE COUNTESS: How dare you!

CHÉRUBIN: Oh, I dare all right! You take her place with the Count. I take his with you – the one most taken in is Figaro.

FIGARO [*aside*]: Scoundrel!

SUZANNE [*aside*]: Cheeky as only a page can be!
  [CHÉRUBIN *attempts to kiss the Countess, the* COUNT *puts himself between them and receives the kiss.*]

THE COUNTESS [*slipping aside*]: Heavens!

FIGARO [*aside – hearing the kiss*]: A nice little girl I was marrying!

CHÉRUBIN [*feeling at the Count's clothes – aside*]: It's His Lordship! [*Runs into pavilion where Marceline and Fanchette are.*]

FIGARO [*coming towards him*]: I'm going to . . .

THE COUNT [*thinking he is talking to the page*]: Since you aren't repeating the kiss . . . [*Aims a blow at him.*]

FIGARO [*who receives it*]: Ah!

THE COUNT: That's one paid off.

FIGARO [*aside as he rubs his cheek*]: Eavesdropping isn't all fun.

SUZANNE [*laughing out loud from the other side of the stage*]: Ha, ha, ha!

THE COUNT [*to the Countess, whom he takes for Suzanne*]: What can one make of this page! He gets a slap like that and goes off laughing.

FIGARO [*aside*]: If he'd got the one that I got –

THE COUNT: I can't take a step without ... but let's forget all this nonsense. He'll spoil all the pleasure of finding you here.

THE COUNTESS [*pretending to talk like Suzanne*]: Were you expecting to?

THE COUNT: After your clever message! [*Takes her hand.*] You are trembling.

THE COUNTESS: I was frightened!

THE COUNT: I didn't mean you to forgo a kiss because I got his.

THE COUNTESS: What liberties!

FIGARO [*aside*]: You hussy!

SUZANNE [*aside*]: Charming!

THE COUNT [*taking her hand*]: What a lovely skin! Would the Countess had such a hand!

THE COUNTESS [*aside*]: How little you know!

THE COUNT: Or an arm so firm and rounded! Or such pretty fingers!

THE COUNTESS [*counterfeiting Suzanne's voice*]: Is this how love ...

THE COUNT: Love is no more than the story of one's heart; pleasure is the reality that brings me to your feet. ...

THE COUNTESS: Don't you love her any more?

THE COUNT: Very much – but three years of marriage makes it seem so respectable.

THE COUNTESS: What did you seek in her?

THE COUNT: What I find in you, my beautiful one.

THE COUNTESS: Such as?

THE COUNT: I don't know. More variety perhaps ... more liveliness of manner, some indefinable quality that constitutes charm: an occasional rebuff perhaps? How do I know? Our wives think they do all that is necessary in loving us. Once it's settled that they love us – they go on doing so. *How* they go on! (Assuming they do love us!) They are so complaint, so acquiescent – always and all the time, until one fine day one is surprised to find satiety where one looked for happiness.

THE COUNTESS [*aside*]: Ah! What a lesson!

THE COUNT: The truth is, Suzie, I have thought many a time that, if we husbands pursue elsewhere the pleasure which eludes us with our wives, it's because they don't give enough attention to the art of holding our interest, of renewing affection, and, so to speak, reviving the charm of possession with the spice of variety.

THE COUNTESS: So it all rests with them?

THE COUNT [*laughing*]: Certainly it doesn't rest with us! Can we change the order of nature? Our part is to win them – theirs –

THE COUNTESS: Theirs?

THE COUNT: Is to keep us. It's too often forgotten.

THE COUNTESS: *I* shan't forget it.

THE COUNT: Nor *I*!

FIGARO [*aside*]: Nor *I*!

SUZANNE [*aside*]: Nor *I*!

THE COUNT [*taking his wife's hand*]: There's an echo somewhere about. We mustn't speak so loud. You don't need to worry, you whom love has so endowed with life and with beauty. Just a dash of caprice and you would be the most provoking of mistresses. [*Kisses her forehead.*] My Suzanne – a Castilian's word is his bond. Here is the gold I promised for the re-purchase of the right I no longer enjoy to the delicious moment you are going to accord me. But, because the grace with which you accord it is beyond price, I add to it this brilliant to wear for love of me.

THE COUNTESS [*curtseying*]: Suzanne accepts all that you offer.

FIGARO [*aside*]: Could depravity go farther?

SUZANNE [*aside*]: So much more grist to the mill.

THE COUNT [*aside*]: She's mercenary. So much the better.

THE COUNTESS [*looking upstage*]: I see torches.

THE COUNT: It's the people preparing for your marriage celebrations. We'll go in one of these pavilions and let them pass by.

THE COUNTESS: Without a light?

THE COUNT: Why not? We aren't going to read!

FIGARO: Upon my word, she's going in! I might have known it!

[*Comes forward.*]

THE COUNT [*in a commanding tone*]: Who goes there?

FIGARO: I'm not going. I'm coming.

THE COUNT: It's Figaro! [*Flies.*]

THE COUNTESS: I'll follow you.

[*She goes into the pavilion on the right, while the* COUNT *disappears among the trees.*]

FIGARO [*still thinking the Countess was Suzanne, trying to see where they have gone*]: I hear nothing now. They've gone in and there it is! [*In an altered voice*] You foolish husbands who rely on hired investigators and spend months struggling with your suspicions and never arriving at any certainty – why don't you follow my example? From the very outset I follow my wife, I listen and immediately know all there is to know. Charming! No doubts, no suspicions! I know just where I stand. [*Moving quickly*] Fortunately I don't mind in the least, her trickery doesn't touch me at all. But now I have got them . . .

SUZANNE [*coming forward in the dark – aside*]: You shall pay for these suspicions. [*Imitating the Countess*] Who goes there?

FIGARO [*wildly*]: Who goes there! One who heartily wishes that he'd never been born!

SUZANNE [*again as the Countess*]: Why! It's Figaro!

FIGARO [*peering at her*]: Your Ladyship!

SUZANNE: Don't talk so loud.

FIGARO: Ah, Madam! Heaven brings you here at the right moment. Where do you think His Lordship is?

SUZANNE: What does he matter to me? Ungrateful that he is. . . .

FIGARO: And Suzanne – my bride-to-be – where do you think she is?

SUZANNE: Not so loud.

FIGARO: That Suzie whom I thought so virtuous, who pretended to be so modest . . . they are in there together. . . . I'm going to call . . .

SUZANNE [*putting her hand over her mouth and forgetting to disguise her voice*]: Don't!

FIGARO: It's Suzie. God damn!

SUZANNE [*in the Countess's voice*]: You seem distraught.

FIGARO [*aside*]: The traitress! She's trying to trick me.

SUZANNE: We must have our revenge, Figaro.

FIGARO: You really want it?

SUZANNE: I shouldn't be true to my sex if I didn't . . . but men have a hundred ways of . . .

FIGARO [*confidently*]: Madam. We need everyone here. The woman's way – is much the best.

SUZANNE [*aside*]: How I'll wallop him!

FIGARO [*aside*]: It would be a lark if before the marriage . . .

SUZANNE: But what sort of revenge is it that a little love won't add spice to?

FIGARO: Though love may not be visible, it may well be concealed under the cloak of deference.

SUZANNE [*hurt*]: I don't know whether you really think that but it's not nice of you to say it.

FIGARO [*with a comic pretence of emotion – on his knees*]: Ah, Madam, I adore you! Consider the time and the place and the circumstances – and may your resentment make up for any graces my supplications may lack!

SUZANNE [*aside*]: My hand is itching!

FIGARO [*aside*]: My heart is pounding.

SUZANNE: But, Sir, have you considered?

FIGARO: Yes, Madam, I have considered.

SUZANNE: That where anger and love are concerned . . .

FIGARO: He who hesitates is lost. Your hand, Madam?

SUZANNE [*in her natural voice – giving him a smack*]: There it is!

FIGARO: Oh *demonio*! What a clout!

SUZANNE: Then what about this one? [*Gives him another.*]

FIGARO: Oh! What's this? The devil! What do you think you are doing? Beating carpets?

SUZANNE [*hitting him at each phrase*]: 'Oh! What's this?' It's me – Suzanne. There's one for your suspicions and one for your revenge, and another for your treachery and your tricks and your insults and all that you were going to do! Is that the way you love me? How does it square with the way you talked this morning?

FIGARO: Ah! Santa Barbara! Yes – it's love all right! Oh happiness! Oh, a hundred times happy Figaro! Keep it up, my darling! Beat me to your heart's content. But when you've beaten me black and blue give a kind glance, Suzie, to the luckiest man who was ever beaten by the hand of a woman!

SUZANNE: The luckiest man! You scoundrel! And yet you didn't hesitate to try it on with the Countess and with such a farrago of specious nonsense that, forgetting who I was, it really was on her behalf that I yielded.

FIGARO: And do you think I could mistake your own lovely voice?

SUZANNE [*laughing*]: You recognized me? Oh! How I'll get my own back yet.

FIGARO: You give a fellow a hiding and yet bear malice; that's just like a woman! But do explain how I came to find you here, when I thought you were with him: why these clothes which misled me and now prove your innocence?

SUZANNE: Ah! You are the innocent! You walk straight into the trap laid for someone else. Is it our fault – if we try to muzzle one fox and catch two?

FIGARO: Well, who's caught the other fellow?

SUZANNE: His wife.

FIGARO: His wife?

SUZANNE: His wife!

FIGARO [*wildly*]: Ah Figaro! Go hang yourself! Fancy not twigging that! His wife? Oh! The cunning – the infinite cunning of women. And so the kisses I heard in this alley –

SUZANNE: Were bestowed on Her Ladyship.

FIGARO: And the page's?

SUZANNE: On His Lordship.

FIGARO: And earlier – behind the sofa.

SUZANNE: On nobody.

FIGARO: Are you sure?

SUZANNE [*laughing*]: You are asking for another smack, Figaro!

FIGARO [*kissing her hand*]: I treasure every single one. But the one the Count gave was in earnest.

SUZANNE: There you go again! On your knees!

FIGARO: I deserve it! On my knees! I crawl. I grovel! [*He does so.*]

SUZANNE [*laughing*]: Ah! The poor Count! What a lot of trouble he's gone to. . . .

FIGARO [*getting up*]: To achieve the conquest of his own wife.

[*The* COUNT *appears upstage.*]

THE COUNT [*to himself*]: I can't find her anywhere in the wood. Perhaps she's here.

SUZANNE [*whispering to Figaro*]: Here he comes!

THE COUNT [*opening the door to the pavilion*]: Suzie, are you there?

FIGARO [*whispering*]: He's looking for *her* – and I thought –

SUZANNE: He hasn't recognized her.

FIGARO: Shall we go through with it? [*Kisses her hand.*]

THE COUNT: A man on his knees to the Countess! Ah, and I'm without my sword. . . . [*Comes downstage.*]

FIGARO [*getting up and speaking in an assumed voice*]: Forgive me, Madam, I had not realized that our usual rendezvous was chosen for the wedding party. . . .

THE COUNT: The man in the dressing-room this morning! [*Strikes his forehead.*]

FIGARO [*as before*]: But let it not be said that such a stupid obstacle came between us and our pleasures.

THE COUNT [*aside*]: Hell! Death! Damnation!

FIGARO [*leading her towards the pavilion, whispering*]: He's blaspheming. [*Aloud*] Let us hurry, Madam, and make up for what we missed when I had to jump from the window.

THE COUNT [*aside*]: Ah! Now we know all!

SUZANNE [*near the left-hand pavilion*]: Before we go in make sure that we aren't followed. [*Kisses Figaro's forehead.*]

THE COUNT [*shouting*]: Vengeance!

[SUZANNE *runs into the pavilion where Fanchette, Marceline, and Chérubin are. The* COUNT *seizes Figaro's arm.*]

FIGARO [*with exaggerated alarm*]: The Master!

THE COUNT [*recognizing him*]: Ah! You dog, it's you, is it? Hello, there! Hello everybody!

[*Enter* PEDRILLO, *booted and spurred.*]

PEDRILLO: My Lord! I find you at last!

THE COUNT: Good. It's Pedrillo. Are you alone?

PEDRILLO: Just back post-haste from Seville.

THE COUNT: Come here! Shout as loudly as you can!

PEDRILLO [*bawling at the top of his voice*]: Not a sign of the page anywhere. Here's the packet.

THE COUNT [*pushing him away*]: Ah! You stupid fool!

PEDRILLO: Your Lordship told me to shout.

THE COUNT [*still hanging on to Figaro*]: For help I meant! Hello there! Anyone who can hear me – come quickly!

PEDRILLO: There's already Figaro and me! How many more do you want?

[*Enter running* BRID'OISON, BAZILE, BARTHOLO, ANTONIO, GRIPE-SOLEIL, *all the wedding party with torches.*]

BARTHOLO [*to Figaro*]: You see – as soon as you gave us the the signal . . .

THE COUNT [*indicating the pavilion on his left*]: Pedrillo – guard that door. . . .

BAZILE [*whispering to Figaro*]: Did you catch him with Suzanne?

THE COUNT [*pointing to Figaro*]: You, my vassals – surround this man for me. You shall answer to me for his life!

BAZILE: Ha, ha!

THE COUNT [*furious*]: Silence! [*To Figaro in an icy tone*] Now, Sir, answer my questions!

FIGARO [*coolly*]: How could I do otherwise, My Lord! You command everything here – except yourself.

THE COUNT: Except myself!

ANTONIO: Now that's talking!

THE COUNT [*furious again*]: If anything could add to my fury it's this calm collected air of his.

FIGARO: Are we soldiers to kill or be killed for causes we know nothing of? For my part I like to know what I'm angry about.

THE COUNT [*beside himself*]: Outrageous! [*Controlling him-*

self] So you pretend you don't know, sir! Be good enough at any rate to say who is the lady you have brought to this pavilion?

FIGARO [*maliciously indicating the other one*]: That one?

THE COUNT [*sharply*]: This one!

FIGARO [*coldly*]: Oh, that's different. A lady who honours me with particular marks of her affection.

BAZILE [*astounded*]: Ha, ha!

THE COUNT: You hear him, Gentlemen?

BARTHOLO [*astounded*]: We hear him.

THE COUNT: And has the lady any other commitments that you are aware of?

FIGARO [*coldly*]: I know that a certain nobleman was interested in her once, but whether he has given her up or she prefers me to a man with greater advantages – she accords me the preference *now*.

THE COUNT [*sharply*]: The preference! [*Controlling himself*] At any rate he's open about it. He admits, gentlemen, what I assure you I have heard from the lips of his accomplice.

BRID'OISON [*stupefied*]: Ac-com-plice!

THE COUNT [*furious*]: When dishonour is flaunted openly the punishment must be similarly proclaimed. [*He goes into the pavilion.*]

ANTONIO: That's fair and proper.

BRID'OISON [*to Figaro*]: W-which has taken the other's wife?

FIGARO [*laughing*]: Neither has had that particular pleasure.

THE COUNT [*heard talking inside the pavilion and dragging someone out*]: All your efforts are in vain. You are lost, Madam! Your hour is come! [*He hasn't looked to see who it is.*] How fortunate that no pledge of so detestable union . . .

FIGARO [*crying out*]: Chérubin!

THE COUNT: My page!

BAZILE: Ha, ha!

THE COUNT [*aside, and beside himself*]: Always this confounded page! What were *you* doing in there?

CHÉRUBIN [*timidly*]: Keeping out of your sight as you told
me to.

PEDRILLO: And I ruined a good horse!

THE COUNT: You go in, Antonio, and bring forth for judgement the infamous creature who has dishonoured me.

BRID'OISON: Is it Her La-Ladyship you are seeking?

ANTONIO: It would serve you right. You've done it yourself
often enough.

THE COUNT [*furious*]: Get in!
   [ANTONIO *goes in*.]

THE COUNT: You will see, gentlemen, that he wasn't alone.

CHÉRUBIN: My lot would have been unendurable had no
kind-hearted person sweetened the bitterness for me. . . .

ANTONIO [*dragging someone out*]: Come on, Madam. No use
begging to be left inside – everybody knows you went in.

FIGARO [*crying out*]: My little cousin!

THE COUNT: Fanchette!

ANTONIO: Ah! *Sacramento!* That *is* kind of His Lordship!
Fancy choosing me to show that it was my own daughter
that was causing the trouble.

THE COUNT [*outraged*]: Who was to know *she* was there!
   [*Makes to go in himself*.]

BARTHOLO: Allow me, Your Excellency. This is all most
bewildering. I'm less excitable. . . . [*He goes in*.]

BRID'OISON: Quite a complicated b-business.

BARTHOLO [*talking to someone as he brings her out*]: Fear nothing, Madam, I'll do you no harm, I promise you. . . .
Marceline!

BAZILE: Ha, ha!

FIGARO: Ha! What a joke! My mother's in it as well!

ANTONIO: So much the worse.

THE COUNT: What do I care about her? The Countess . . .

[SUZANNE *comes out with her fan over her face.*]

Ah, here she comes! [*He seizes her violently by the arm.*] Gentlemen! What do you think should be done with this odious –

[SUZANNE *falls on her knees, still looking down.*]

THE COUNT: No, no!

[FIGARO *throws himself on his knees at the other side.*]

THE COUNT [*louder*]: No, no!

[*All fall on their knees, except Brid'oison.*]

THE COUNT: Not if there were a hundred of you!

[*The* COUNTESS *emerges from the other pavilion.*]

THE COUNTESS [*throwing herself on her knees*]: Allow me to
join you.

THE COUNT [*looking from Suzanne to the Countess*]: Ah! Whatever is this?

BRID'OISON [*laughing*]: B-by Jove! It's Her Ladyship!

THE COUNT [*endeavouring to raise her*]: What! It was you,
Countess? [*In a supplicating voice*] Only your generous forgiveness . . .

THE COUNTESS [*laughing*]: You'd say, 'No, no!' if you were
in my place. Whereas I for the third time today accord it
unconditionally. [*She rises.*]

SUZANNE: And I too. [*Gets up.*]

MARCELINE: And I too. [*Gets up.*]

FIGARO: And I too. There's an echo somewhere about.
[*They all get up.*]

THE COUNT: An echo! I thought I was being clever and
they've treated me like a child.

THE COUNTESS [*laughing*]: Don't regret it, My Lord!

FIGARO [*dashing his knees with his cap*]: A day's work like this
is good practice for a diplomat.

THE COUNT [*to Suzanne*]: The message you fastened with a pin?

SUZANNE: Her Ladyship dictated it.

THE COUNT: Then the reply should be made to her. [*Kisses
her hand.*]

THE COUNTESS: Everyone shall have his own. [*She gives the purse to Figaro and the diamond to Suzanne.*]

SUZANNE [*to Figaro*]: Another dowry.

FIGARO [*slapping the purse with his hand*]: And of the three this took most getting.

SUZANNE: Like our marriage.

GRIPE-SOLEIL: And the marriage garter – can I have it?

THE COUNTESS [*throws the ribbon which she has taken from her bodice*]: The garter. It was with her clothes. Here it is.

CHÉRUBIN [*who is quickest to pick it up*]: I defy anyone to get it from me!

THE COUNT [*laughing*]: How did you like the smack on the ear you got a little while ago?

CHÉRUBIN [*recoiling and half drawing his sword*]: I got?

FIGARO [*miming his discomfort*]: He got it on *my* ear! That's how great men dispense justice.

THE COUNT [*laughing*]: *You* got it? Ah! What do you say to that, my dear?

THE COUNTESS [*absorbed in her thoughts, but replying with fervour*]: Ah, yes, dear for ever and ever, I assure you.

THE COUNT [*slapping the judge on the shoulder*]: And you, Brid'oison – what's your opinion?

BRID'OISON: What's my opinion, Your Lordship? All I can say is – I don't know what to think!

ALL: A very sensible verdict!

FIGARO: I was poor and people despised me. I showed some evidence of ability and got myself disliked for it. Now, with a pretty wife and a fortune . . .

THE COUNT: Everyone will be your friend.

FIGARO: Can that really be?

BARTHOLO: I know them.

FIGARO [*to the audience*]: My wife and my fortune apart – You will, I am sure, do me honour. . . .

[*All join in singing and dancing.*]

BAZILE [*sings*]:

> Triple dowry, charming wife,
> What a start for married life.
> A noble Lord – a beardless boy!
> Such rivals only fools annoy.
> The clever man for all they say
> In the end will get his way.

FIGARO: I know. [*Sings*]

> Let those who are well born rejoice.

BAZILE: No. [*Sings*]

> Let those who are well found rejoice.

SUZANNE:

> Let a husband break his vows
> It's just a joke the world allows –
> But should a wife like freedom take
> The world will punish her mistake.
> The strong it is for all they say
> Who in the end will have their way.

FIGARO:

> Many a man who takes a wife
> Thinks to lead a quiet life.
> He keeps a watchdog – silly man
> To guard his house – as if he can.
> For woman's love – for all they say
> Finds the means to fly away.

BRID'OISON [*sings*]:

> G-gentlemen, you've seen our play
> What it's worth you best can say.
> In one respect it's true to life
> All the fuss, the hubbub – strife,
> In the end – for all they say
> Are but follies of a day.

CURTAIN

NOTES ON THE CHARACTERS AND
THEIR COSTUMES

Printed by Beaumarchais in the first editions of *The Barber of Seville* (1775) and *The Marriage of Figaro* (1785).

THE BARBER OF SEVILLE

The costumes should all be in the Old Spanish style.

COUNT ALMAVIVA, Spanish grandee and Rosine's unknown lover. He appears in the first act in a coat and breeches of satin, a voluminous brown cloak or Spanish cape, a black hat with a coloured ribbon and turned-down brim; in the second act in a trooper's uniform and riding boots and wearing moustaches. In the third act he appears as a student with hair cut round, a deep ruff, short coat, trousers, stockings, and clerical cloak; in the fourth he is splendidly attired in the Spanish manner with a rich mantle and the full brown cloak which he gathers about him.

BARTHOLO, a doctor and Rosine's guardian. He wears a black coat, short with buttons, a full wig, ruff and turned-back cuffs, a black waist band, and, when he is going out, a red cloak.

ROSINE, a young lady of noble birth, ward of Bartholo. She is dressed in the Spanish fashion.

FIGARO, Barber of Seville, wears the costume of a Spanish dandy, his head covered with a *redecilla* or Spanish hair net, a white hat with coloured ribbon, a lace neckerchief very loosely knotted, waistcoat and breeches of satin with silver buttons and frogs of silver braid, a broad silk sash, garters with tassels on each leg, jacket in contrasting colour with facings the same colour as the waistcoat, white stockings and grey shoes.

DON BAZILE, organist and Rosine's singing master, wears a black hat with flat brim, short cassock, and long cloak without neck or wrist bands.

LA JEUNESSE (YOUTHFUL), Bartholo's aged manservant.

L'ÉVEILLÉ (WAKEFUL), Bartholo's other manservant, a dull, sleepy boy. Both wear Galician costume, hair in pigtails, buff waistcoat, wide leather belt with buckles, short trousers, and jacket with wide open sleeves allowing freedom to the arms.

A notary.

An alcalde, a beadle carrying a large white staff in his hand.

Several alguazils and servants carrying torches.

The scene is set in Seville, in the street beneath the windows of Rosine's room in the first act and for the remainder of the play in a room in Bartholo's house.

THE MARRIAGE OF FIGARO

COUNT ALMAVIVA should be played with great dignity yet with grace and affability. The depravity of his morals should in no way detract from the elegance of his manners. It was customary in those days for great noblemen to treat any design upon the fair sex in a spirit of levity. The part is all the more difficult to play well in that it is always the unsympathetic role. Nevertheless, played by an excellent actor [Monsieur Molé], it brought out the qualities of the other roles and assured the success of the play.

In the first and second acts Almaviva wears hunting costume and high boots in the Spanish style, in the third and succeeding acts, a splendid costume in the same style.

THE COUNTESS. Torn between two conflicting emotions she should display only a restrained tenderness and very moderate degree of resentment, above all nothing which might impair her amiable and virtuous character in the eyes of the audience. This role, one of the most difficult in the play, brought out fully the distinguished talents of Mlle Saint-Val, the younger.

The Countess appears in the first, second, third, fourth acts in a loose wrap with no hair ornaments. She is at home and supposedly indisposed. In the fifth act she wears Suzanne's dress and high *coiffure*.

FIGARO. One cannot too strongly recommend the actor who plays this role to get right into the part as did Monsieur Dazincourt.

If he sees in it anything other than good sense seasoned with gaiety and sallies of wit – above all, if he introduces any element of caricature – he will diminish the effect of a role which, in the opinion of Monsieur Préville, the leading comic actor of our theatre, would bring honour to the talents of any player able to appreciate the fine shades of the part and fully rise to the opportunities it offers.

The Costume is as in *The Barber of Seville*.

SUZANNE. She is a resourceful, intelligent, and lively young woman, but she has none of the almost brazen gaiety characteristic of some of our young actresses who play maidservants. The charm of her character is indicated in the preface,* and the actress who has not seen Mlle Contat should study it if she wishes to play the part to advantage.

Her dress in the first four acts is a plain white bodice, decorated in the Basque fashion, very elegant, her skirt the same, and she wears a *toque* of the kind which our milliners call '*a la Suzanne*'.

In the celebration in the fourth act the Count places on her head a chaplet with a long veil, plumes, and white ribbons. In the fifth act she wears her Mistress's gown and no hair ornament.

MARCELINE. She is a woman of intelligence and of naturally lively temperament but the errors of her youth and subsequent experience have chastened her. If the actress who plays the part can rise with a proper proud defiance to the moral heights of the third act, after the recognition scene, she will add greatly to the interest of the work. Her dress is that of a duenna, modest in colour with a black hat.

ANTONIO. He need show no more than a moderate degree of tipsiness which passes off by degrees so that by the fifth act it is no longer noticed.

FANCHETTE. She is a young girl about twelve years old, very naïve. Her dress is a plain brown bodice with silver buttons and braid: her skirt is a contrasting colour and she wears a small black hat with feathers – like the other peasant girls – at the wedding.

* Beaumarchais defended himself, his play, and his characters against the critics in a long preface, which in fact says nothing about the character of Suzanne which is not implicit in the play.

CHERUBIN. This part can only be played, as it was in fact, by a young and very pretty woman: we have no very young men in our theatre who are at the same time sufficiently mature to appreciate the fine points of the part. Chérubin is diffident in the extreme in the presence of the Countess but otherwise he is a charming young scamp. The basis of his character is an undefined and restless desire. He is entering on adolescence all unheeding and with no understanding of what is happening to him, and throws himself eagerly into everything that comes along. In fact, he is what every mother, in her innermost heart, would wish her own son to be even though he might give her much cause for suffering.

His rich costume in the first and second acts is that of a page at the Spanish court, white embroidered in silver. He wears a light blue cloak off the shoulder: his hat is much be-plumed.

In the fourth act he has the same bodice, skirt, and hat as the young peasants who bring him in.

In the fifth act, officer's uniform, cockade, and sword.

BARTHOLO. The character and dress are as in *The Barber of Seville*. The role is of secondary importance.

BAZILE. The character and dress are as in *The Barber of Seville*. Also of secondary importance.

BRID'OISON should display the honest and frank confidence of the beasts of the field who have lost their shyness. His stammer is very much part of him and we should hardly be aware of it. The actor will be making a grave mistake and be playing the part in quite the wrong way if he deliberately sets out to be funny. The point lies in the contrast between the dignity of his position and the innate absurdity of his character. The less the actor caricatures it the better he will demonstrate his skill.

DOUBLEMAIN. He is dressed like the judge but his white staff is shorter.

The usher and alguazil. They wear uniform, cloak, sword – after the manner of the comic valet, but the sword is worn at the side without a leather belt. They do not wear high boots but black shoes, white wig with long curls, and carry a short white staff.

NOTES ON THE CHARACTERS AND THEIR COSTUMES

GRIPE-SOLEIL. Peasant costume, loose sleeves, coloured coat, white hat.

Young shepherdess. Dress like that of Fanchette.

PEDRILLO. Coat, waistcoat, sash, whip and riding boots, horseman's hat.

Characters without speaking parts. Some as judges, others as peasants, others again in livery.